ACHIEVING
EQUITY
in Gifted Programming

What the Experts Say

"In order to see a child's true potential, they must be exposed to intellectual opportunities that are appropriated to their level and background, and build off their experiences. Our talent development program has been a gamechanger for our students from underserved populations because it has provided each child the opportunity to access higher order thinking skills. With these skills, students begin to tap into their true potential, which otherwise may have gone unnoticed."

— Carmela Riley, District U-46

"April Wells, an award-winning educator and leader, has a long track record of breaking down barriers to talent development for *all* of our children. Her unique combination of practical experience, knowledge of the research and literature, and fierce advocacy has resulted in a first-rate resource for educators, families, and policymakers. I highly recommend this book for anyone interested in improving how we approach advanced education."

— Jonathan A. Plucker, Ph.D., Johns Hopkins University

"April's mission to establish equitable access to gifted education arises from her own very personal journey. Her informed perspective as a young student, a teacher, a parent, and now as an adult educational leader fuels her tireless efforts to remove barriers for all high-potential students. She urges us to honor all students, their original language, and the culture from which they come in exposing them to enrichment and providing access to academic challenge. April's call to focus on local norms and local needs, along with high support balanced with high expectations, compels us to embrace the inevitable, but necessary, discomfort inherent in changing current educational systems."

— Julie Luck Jensen, Past President of Illinois Association for Gifted Children

"April Wells brings authentic, 'boots on the ground' experience to this book, having created multiple programs for children who are often overlooked for gifted education services. Her work comes together in the AIM program, which increases access to gifted programs by focusing on cultivating higher level thinking skills in young children. This program is consistent with a talent development approach to gifted education that emphasizes alternative identification methods, talent spotting, early intervention, and enrichment."

— Paula Olszewski-Kubilius, Ph.D., Northwestern University

ACHIEVING EQUITY
in Gifted Programming

April Wells

PRUFROCK PRESS INC.
WACO, TEXAS

Library of Congress Control Number:2019955613

Copyright ©2020, Prufrock Press Inc.

Edited by Katy McDowall

Cover and layout design by Allegra Denbo

ISBN-13: 978-1-61821-877-3

Printed in the United States of America.

At the time of this book's publication, all facts and figures cited are the most current available. All telephone numbers, addresses, and website URLs are accurate and active. All publications, organizations, websites, and other resources exist as described in the book, and all have been verified. The author and Prufrock Press Inc. make no warranty or guarantee concerning the information and materials given out by organizations or content found at websites, and we are not responsible for any changes that occur after this book's publication. If you find an error, please contact Prufrock Press Inc.

Prufrock Press Inc.
P.O. Box 8813
Waco, TX 76714-8813
Phone: (800) 998-2208
Fax: (800) 240-0333
http://www.prufrock.com

Dedication

To Charles, Kennedy, Sydney, and Geneva, my life is better because of your presence. Endless thanks for being the source of my motivation. Charles, I am grateful for your strength and resolve that, at times, carried me through this process when I wanted to quit. Your reassurance and support provided a mirror for me to reflect to see what is truly inside me. To Kennedy, Sydney, and Geneva, I hope my willingness to pursue my passion will incite an insatiable desire in each of you to achieve greater than your hearts could ever imagine.

Table of Contents

Acknowledgments

Writing this book caused me to believe in myself on a level that I had not tapped in recent years. In the face of the unknown—this is my first book, unless you count the young author books I wrote in elementary school—I embraced extreme discomfort and equally compelling joy. I learned how to give myself grace. I owe a great deal of thanks and gratitude to two pillars in my life, who, although they were not here to witness my work, are vitally connected to everything I have been able to achieve. I believe they had an idea how my story would unfold. Thank you to my Nanos, my grandmother, and Larry, my uncle, for always believing in me, helping me to see beyond limitations, and simply (yet most notably) being there. And, to my parents who gave me a gift that set this plan in motion, thanks for life, love, and support.

My experience as an educator brings a smile to many faces, but one face in particular is marked with distinction in my memory. I will forever be grateful for the late Ronald O'Neal, Sr., (Papi) for encouraging me to pursue my leadership degree in education. Without his guidance, I never would have come close to touching the work in gifted education in the way I have been able to. He encouraged me to obtain my leadership degree so that, whenever an opportunity presented itself, I would ready. Thanks to him, when gifted education called, I was able to answer.

To my dearest friend, Amber, whose friendship has translated into family, your encouragement at the onset of this experience gave me freedom to take the risk. Guess what? I finished the book. Our friendship is truly a gift that keeps on giving. You along with Traci and Carolyn (Nani) are the most prominent cultural brokers I know, bridging experiences for a little girl who grew up in poverty but was not poor.

Thank you to my mentor, Julie Luck Jensen, who recognized my spark for gifted education and fanned it by encouraging me to present at staff meetings, attend an Illinois Association for Gifted Children conference, and go to my first National Association for Gifted Children annual convention. Thank you also for being my first consultant. You have been a great resource for my endless questions and an even better friend.

My work is central to me, and it is about making withdrawals from deposits that so many others have made into me. To that end, I would like to thank Paula Olszewski-Kubilius, Ph.D., and Rhoda Rosen, Ph.D., for partnering with me through the Center for Talent Development at Northwestern University to bring innovative programs to District U-46 and to hundreds of students who remind me of my younger self.

When I returned to District U-46 to work on the gifted charter, I was fortunate to meet some amazing friends. I am thankful for the loving guidance from Barbara Johnson in helping me to grow into my leadership disposition.

Thanks to my tribe of educators, students, parents, and stakeholders of District U-46, who also beat the equity drum that creates a sound that sustains us as we work.

I would also like to thank Joel McIntosh, Katy McDowall, and the team at Prufrock Press for opening doors for this timely and timeless conversation about equity in gifted education to be taken to more extensive platforms.

May we all continue to be a voice for those whose anguish and tears go unheard.

Introduction

This book represents an intersection of both theory and practice on how educators can respond to the disproportionate participation of culturally, linguistically, and economically diverse (CLED) students in gifted education programs. Much of what is shared originates from my cumulative experience during my tenure as a gifted administrator in Illinois. Research on talent development as an instructional intervention, cultural awareness, and social justice in education converges and supports the establishment of inclusive gifted programs. Including research and implementation considerations, *Achieving Equity in Gifted Education* offers educators a platform to address underrepresentation. Each chapter poses an opportunity for educators to address their own understanding of CLED learners in gifted education and to disrupt a problem that has plagued the field for decades.

The school environment and experiences in which students partake are correlated to academic gains. An effective environment and challenging experiences are particularly important for students from diverse backgrounds. Enhancing access to rigorous learning environments fuels the growth of equity in gifted education. Disproportionate participation in gifted education can be viewed as a social justice issue that plagues the nation, but educators can redesign practices and policies in order for gifted programming to adequately represent the students whom educators are responsible for serving. Providing greater access to gifted education for advanced youth benefits not only their academic growth, but also their psychosocial development.

There is a gifted gap (Yaluma & Tyner, 2018). Each at-potential student not adequately served by gifted programming represents potential that is lost and assesses a tax paid by the nation. The absence of bright, diverse learners in the nation's classrooms represents lost opportunities. Brains are malleable. Students from all backgrounds start off at commensurate levels of innovation and questioning ability, but the longer they are in school, CLED students fall behind. Educators recognize the limits of some students' backgrounds, but that does not absolve educators of their responsibility to reflect on how to cultivate talent in students from *all* backgrounds.

Underrepresentation in gifted programming can be addressed; it does not have to go on in perpetuity. This work is positioned at a critical junction in gifted education. When the population of students identified for gifted services is juxtaposed against the nation's demographics, the cry to respond is resounding. Addressing equitable access to gifted programs is essential. The public education system has a notable role to play in equalizing opportunities in gifted education for students from marginalized groups. Across the nation, students with equal talents experience unequal outcomes. Educators and other stakeholders in the field recognize the problem—and there have been some successful approaches—but there is still considerable work to do. Educators' investment has been noted, but those in the gifted education field have not always embarked upon the necessary steps to further the conversation into more involved commitment that translates into sustainable action. The pursuit of equity means that program administrators must be cognizant of the barriers to gifted identification. The following barriers to identification are addressed throughout this text: English as a second language (ESL), referral or nomination processes (e.g., two-phase identification systems), identification procedures, previous learning, cultural conflict, and biases.

Uncovering blind spots and understanding gifted students through a culturally aware lens are critical to addressing underrepresentation. Recognizing blind spots in gifted education requires robust attention. Understanding the intersection of poverty and race is also central to addressing equity in gifted programs. Although poverty is not the only reason for students being excluded from gifted programs, it is a prominent issue in the discussion of disproportionality. Income inequities exacerbate underrepresentation. Note, however, that poverty is palatable, and it is easier for educators to view poverty as a source of disproportionality, but there is more to underrepresentation than poverty. There is a cultural perception gap that also impedes minority students from being identified for gifted programming. This gap represents the faulty way in which educators view students. The cultural conflict that arises from not fully understanding the differences may lead educators to have erroneous views of students from diverse backgrounds. These views may dictate educators' interactions, beliefs, and thoughts about students. Culturally proficient educators recognize the danger of such blind spots. From the research-based programming implementations described in this text—as well as further work and reflection—educators will be able to uncover blind spots and develop their skills in understanding students through a culturally responsive lens, permitting students from all backgrounds to access gifted programming.

CHAPTER 1

Underrepresentation

How Did We Get Here?

Equity, access, and culturally responsive pedagogy are the banquet chicken of public education. These educational underpinnings are on the menu everywhere, but rarely done right. They are so widely available that when they are not done right, no alarms are signaled. But when equity is addressed effectively, the educator workforce is strengthened in its collective knowledge, skills, and practices to be an inclusive and culturally responsive system. What comes to mind when you hear the terms *equity* and *equality*? Equity and equality are not synonymous. Equality, or equal treatment, means that all students get the same support. Equity is achieved by all students receiving the individual supports that they need in order to fully access the learning environment. To extend the conversation, consider an additional component—justice. Justice is all students fully accessing appropriate services because causes of inequity were addressed. In many situations, this means that privilege was recognized and that barriers were eradicated. Underrepresentation can best be addressed through efforts aimed at dismantling systemic barriers.

Districts should replicate models of equity and access when they see them implemented properly. These transformative practices are necessary in order to adequately serve a wider span of students. The benefits to educators, which enhance their practice, would be notable. A culturally proficient workforce is necessary to meet the needs of all of the students and families. School districts across America have goals and mission statements that rightfully include equity and access in gifted education. An unfortunate reality about gifted programs is that they have largely been a platform to maintain segregated school environments. Gifted education is at a significant crossroads. The unintended consequences of unequal outcomes can be remedied, and addressing this problem of practice will have significant impact. Ultimately, the racial disparities in gifted education can widen long-term gaps in opportunity. Participation in gifted programs positions students for positive future outcomes, including improved academic performance, motivation, and classroom engagement.

Although many gifted educators recognize that they have not satisfactorily met the needs of significant portions of student populations, namely students of color, they are determined to continue moving forward with responsive interventions. In the field, there is agreement that underrepresentation does not have to happen. At the risk of preaching to the choir, it is worth noting that even the most skilled choirs rehearse. Although you may not walk away from reading this book with the single remedy to underrepresentation, I anticipate that you will have additional tools to add to your repertoire as you advocate for diverse populations. Advocating for gifted children means advocating for all children. Many undeniably bright students are left out, overlooked, underserved, and left to develop on their own and map their own trajectories.

Advocating for gifted children means advocating for all children.

The issue of inequity in gifted education is not a student problem. Although many interventions consider students from a deficit approach, educators are grossly missing the mark. Inequity is a systemic problem, and educators must undergo a shift in their approach. They have to be thoughtful and methodical, while being bold and confronting this social justice issue. Gifted educators, advocates, and stakeholders must ensure that all gifted students have access and are served. Difficult? Yes. Impossible? No. The accumulated human capital made up of underserved learners represents a significant amount of untapped talent. The following section highlights the impact of implicit bias and privilege on academic experiences for CLED learners. Educators need to see diverse learners as academically worthy and identify interventions to address individual thought patterns, values, and beliefs that run interference in serving diverse learners.

The Impact of Implicit Bias and Privilege

Well-meaning educators have invested significant resources in the development of equity plans—systemic plans aimed at promoting greater access and equity for students from underrepresented backgrounds. Yet, educators still do not uniformly and consistently experience the rates of representation, by diverse learners, in gifted education at rates that mirror the proportion of diverse learners in the population. This costly, unjust mismatch is one of notable proportions. But gifted educators can do something about underrepresentation. They must. Oftentimes when students are overlooked, they do not maximize their potential in general education classrooms. Untapped potential is costly, figuratively and literally. The unparalleled level of personal and professional fortitude necessary for educators to tackle the conversation requires a depth of self-exploration and analysis that can be daunting and is not always easily navigable. Equity leaders run the risk of alienating themselves and jeopardizing their efforts to remedy underrepresentation, appearing disruptive in an already small field within education.

| *Untapped potential is costly,*
figuratively and literally.

The pursuit of equity in gifted education is laden with challenges, but the challenges are surmountable. Educators can mitigate the unequal outcomes in gifted education. In anticipation of working to address underrepresentation, significant thought and attention must be devoted to understanding the origins of underrepresentation. Before this problem can truly be addressed, it has to be thoroughly understood. Gifted educators cannot change the system if they are not willing to acknowledge what they supported that allowed the field to get here. The unveiling of this systemic issue is one that cannot be handled lightly. The best way to understand and remedy underrepresentation is by looking at it from both etic and emic perspectives. The voices of individuals who have firsthand knowledge of underrepresentation as members of marginalized groups lend critical support to the conversation of equity and access in gifted education. There is also opportunity to hear from those who may not be from a marginalized group. They, too, can have invaluable input.

By bringing diversity of thought to the forefront of this issue, educators will be able to engage in a collective lift. This lift will allow educators to design effective gifted education programs and act as agents of change in public education. Ultimately, the result will include the perspectives of those from academia, as well as those who are in the trenches in schools on a daily basis. Combining the strengths and awareness from academia as well as the K–12 system encourages a comprehensive approach. Although academic and K–12 educators employ different strategies, they have the same goal in mind. Raising awareness about the privilege and bias that run rampant through gifted education is not to assign blame or guilt; instead, the motivation is to fully recognize the issues through a problem-solving model.

Countless interventions aimed at remedying underrepresentation do not work because they are not targeted at the root causes of underrepresentation. Educators of all types must acknowledge what led the field of gifted education to this point so that they can assert a degree of certainty, supported by commitment that they will not repeat the atrocities leveraged by underrepresentation. For years, educators in gifted education have addressed symptoms of underrepresentation when they needed to delve into deeper levels of tireless work and address the root cause. To effectively access pipelines of untapped potential, gifted educators must peel back layers in public education and expose blind spots that work to perpetuate racialized outcomes. Gifted education feels the effects of underrepresentation on a daily basis, but educators do not readily assess the cause. Privilege and bias are major barriers for underserved learners. Every human being has biases. The extent to which educators' biases are not checked is what creates challenges in the face of equity pedagogy.

Keep reading! You already bought the book, so you might as well go for the full ride. The discomfort that accompanies this conversation is necessary. I am not asserting that gifted educators are racist; I am posing a big issue for contemplation. The American history of racism and subjugation of Black and minority individuals has always leaked into education, and it must be abated. A primary step is acknowledging the sources that fuel inequity. Otherness strategically divides people. For example, Black people have been subjected to a demoralizing existence, one in which their language, culture, and identity were stripped in an attempt to usurp authority over an entire group of people. The distinctive, entangled historical landscape in the United States regarding race relations has bearing on every facet of life. Black people have a traumatic historical narrative dating back to the earliest accounts of involuntary arrival to America. For a system as inhumane as chattel slavery to be perpetuated, Black people had to be seen as less than, inferior, or other. The sting of this institution has far-reaching consequences. Black Americans still witness the effects of strained race relations from trauma carried out against their ancestors that is still perpetuated today. A group of people minus their identification is subjected to the definitions, constraints, and limits forced upon them by the oppressor. Every system—from law to education to medicine—has significantly constrained the Black experience in America. Fast forward hundreds of years, and the intricacy of a system intended to impugn a group of people is still unrelenting.

There is an urgent need for educators to view diverse learners as academically capable and worthy.

The sting of privilege, bias, and racism has restricted and continues to limit achievement opportunities in education for children of color. There is an urgent need for educators to view diverse learners as academically capable and worthy. In order to facilitate such a change, a substantial mindset shift must take place. Educators must address their thought patterns, values, and beliefs that interfere with identifying and serving diverse learners in gifted education. Educators' values and beliefs intertwine to create policies in gifted education. Policies, gatekeeping systems, and structures that contribute to underrepresentation are at work even while competent educators are at the helm. Gifted education has to be reconsidered. Having good people lead the work is not enough. The work within this systems approach also includes considerable change at the individual level. Educators must be aware of their own culture, recognize their biases, and develop an awareness of diverse cultures, building their cultural proficiency. A worldview that embraces multiculturalism is necessary to effectively serve in public education.

Underrepresentation in Gifted Education

Underrepresentation is a stealthy issue that requires innovative strategies coupled with compassion and willingness to deal with complexities. Every component of a gifted program—from identification and selection, to instructional delivery, curriculum resource selection, and parent outreach—must be reviewed against a school's or district's equity goals. Public schools serve students from all backgrounds. As evidenced in educational outcomes, disproportionality in advanced learning, student discipline, and special education occurs widely. Educators have tremendous work to do in the name of equity in public education. Simply stated, equity means that all students have access to opportunities for a high-quality education. Because giftedness occurs in students from all backgrounds, a school's or district's gifted population should responsively reflect the demographics of the district. Responsive representation is not to be mistaken for perfect proportionality, but the rate of participation should reflect each group's population in the school or district. Educators also must consider how they interact with students from diverse backgrounds. In many instances, student outcomes are directly related to the way students are treated in schools. CLED students experience school differently because of an unfortunate reality—in some instances, educators treat them differently than other students.

Equity means that all students have access to opportunities for a high-quality education.

Whiteness has been normalized, making CLED students subject to a pervasive world of otherness. Otherness ascribes value to Whiteness and asserts it as the norm. Whiteness is a social construct. Otherness deals with the way identities are constructed, particularly majority and minority identities. Although otherness is not natural, it is set up in such a way that it is presumed as natural. Take into consideration the use of checklists in gifted identification. The use of checklists in identifying potentially gifted students as part of a selection or nomination process is widely implemented as a valid method for identifying characteristics of giftedness. Much of what is typically captured in these checklists is an assessment of privilege or access, at best. Culture is inextricably woven into one's identity, and students must be viewed through culturally aware lenses. The reliance on characteristics, viewed in the absence of cultural awareness, perpetuates disproportionate rates of identification for CLED students.

To further complicate the issue, more than 80% of teachers in America are White (Snyder, de Brey, & Dillow, 2019); however, nationally, minority students make up a majority of the population in public schools. Racial diversity has grown more quickly among public school students than among teachers. Having a teaching force that is less racially diverse than its students contributes to underrepresentation. Education experts agree that a racially diverse teaching force is beneficial for students. Research has found that Black teachers have higher expectations for Black students than do White teachers (Gershenson, Holt, & Papageorge, 2016). Perception matters. Black teachers' perceptions of Black students lead these educators to more positively assess how Black students perform in school. The more that Black students' behaviors are seen through culturally proficient lenses, the more those students access opportunities matched to their abilities.

Cultural conflict occurs across the length of the chasm that potentially separates students from the teachers charged with teaching them. For decades, gifted programs have largely served students who are White or Asian—with little diversity. Diversifying gifted programming is a major upset to the status quo; the lack of representation by diverse students in gifted has reached a pinnacle. Efforts from local educators to the national level are raising awareness of the impact of racial diversity in gifted programs. Giftedness knows no boundaries. As detailed in National Association for Gifted Children (NAGC, 2018) task force findings and suggestions, there is a movement to garner support for adequate identification and serving of children from minority groups. Researchers, educators, and practitioners are focusing their energy to identify the most plausible ways to meet the unique needs of all gifted learners, who "come from all racial, ethnic, and cultural populations, as well as all economic strata" (p. 1). Combining understanding from their diverse perspectives, educators have the momentum that is necessary to make a significant dent in underrepresentation.

The degree to which gifted children in poverty and from minority groups are identified and served is a source of dissension. Awareness is instrumental in the development of policies and practices that create supportive environments in which all gifted children can experience the educational environment matched to their needs. Gifted learners may demonstrate early readiness, or their skills may emerge at later times in their academic careers. These learners may bring a wealth of skills that point to high ability, but these skills may not always be assessed or viewed properly in CLED students. Educators tend to view behaviors against a standard of behaviors that are deemed typical, and manifestations that differ from the norm are seen through a deficit lens. There is an expectation that minority students will assimilate into the dominant culture. Rarely do educators look at behaviors, school skills, and readiness through a culturally aware lens. Cultural awareness positions educators to understand more about the extensive wealth that students from diverse populations bring to schools and classrooms on a daily basis. Children from some groups are attending schools where their full identities are not embraced.

Ability has to be viewed within context to follow equity pedagogy. Equity pedagogy involves all students getting what they need in order to fully participate in learning environments. Assumed in equity pedagogy is access. Access refers to the full participation and involvement in the educational environment of all learners. Instruction that reflects equity pedagogy works to resolve the notion of invisibility. Invisibility occurs when students are excluded from gifted and talented programs because of language barriers, socioeconomics, or biases. Demonstrated achievement is a notable construct in identification for gifted programs; in many cases, children of color are left out because achievement is not equally distributed due to barriers that certain groups encounter. If viewed through a narrow perspective laden with biases, implicit or explicit, diverse learners run the risk of remaining invisible in classrooms.

*Access is a critical component
when considering programming
for diverse learners.*

Educators cannot continue business as usual in gifted education. The ultimate effect of invisibility issues pushes students to other dumping grounds in public education. High-potential learners have unique learner profiles; therefore, they require thoughtful, specialized academic programming to meet their academic and social-emotional needs. The opportunity cost for unmet needs in this area is costly. Students—and communities at large—feel the sting of unmet student needs, from the local to global level. High-quality gifted programming can be an answer to this conundrum. Diverse gifted students are unseen, yet they are hidden in plain sight. For example, researchers found that one factor dramatically increased the likelihood that Black students will be placed in a gifted program: Black public school students, who are 54% less likely than their White peers to be identified as eligible for gifted education services, get a clear boost if their teacher is also Black (Nicholson-Crotty, Grissom, Nicholson-Crotty, & Redding, 2016). The researchers found that Black students are 3 times more likely to be placed in a gifted program if they have a Black teacher rather than a White teacher.

Culturally diverse gifted learners experience microaggressions and are ignored by privilege simply because of their race or ethnicity. In many instances, the general education experience is not equally matched to learners' trajectory of growth. This mismatch widens the range of student abilities in the classroom, which curtails the effectiveness of teaching and learning experiences.

The extent to which gifted educators employ inclusive practices aimed at serving culturally diverse, linguistically diverse, and economically vulnerable students needs to increase. Access is a critical component when considering programming for diverse learners. They must have access to environments in which their academic excellence can be nurtured. Access means that students—and their families—have the opportunity to know about gifted services, as well as the school and district processes. In some instances, outreach needs to be differentiated. Families engage in school differently; educators are responsible for communicating through platforms that are conducive to the way families access information. Educators must work to ensure that families' interactions with schools are understandable and accessible regardless of one's cultural and linguistic diversity. Families may need to be guided to understand their students' abilities and necessary educational environment to continue their growth. Students' educational repertoire consists of more than formal teaching and learning experiences in the classroom. Inputs such as previous opportunities for learning, socioeconomics, native language, and access to cultural and social capital influence their demonstrated achievement. As compelling and far-reaching as poverty is, race also presents an equally critical impression on students' learning. The next realm of development in gifted education involves unveiling potential in all promising learners. Their ability must be viewed through a culturally aware worldview. The expectation is not that students rise to academic levels of prominence in the absence of programming before they are served. Giftedness occurs in all racial, linguistic, and socioeconomic groups, and educators' narrow view of exceptionality constrains opportunities for diverse learners. There is an urgency in seeing diverse learners as academically worthy. The place to start is with visibility; educators must see these learners.

REFLECTION QUESTIONS

1. What is the racial makeup of your gifted program? Does that vary when comparing Title I schools and non-title schools?

2. Describe how you would explain underrepresentation in gifted education to someone who does not have an educational background.

3. What practical steps can you take to unveil potential in promising learners in your school or district?

4. What have you done in the name of educational advocacy that breaks down barriers that preclude access for students from underrepresented backgrounds?

5. What barriers to gifted identification exist in your school or district?

CHAPTER 2

Roadmap to Redesign

One District's Story

Culturally, linguistically, and economically diverse learners are disproportionately represented in gifted programs, but there is promise in using responsive practices that allow for more inclusive environments that subsequently afford opportunities to all students. Educators can do something about underrepresentation. Even in the most constrained financial situations, programming or a continuum of services can be implemented to meet the needs of the gifted. Some of the framework considerations that must be addressed in a comprehensive redesign or review of gifted programming include evaluating the local definition of giftedness; program philosophy; mission statement; program components; education for educators, administrators, and parents; and district mindset. This process also involves recognizing the barriers that exist and dismantling them in the spirit of equity and excellence in gifted education. Many of these considerations are outlined in this chapter as a part of one district's redesign.

District U-46

Situated outside of the city of Chicago, in the northwest suburbs, is the second largest school district in the state of Illinois. The district serves students from 11 communities across 90 square miles. The attendance areas covered in the boundaries of the district are diverse in all aspects, a fact that is celebrated in the district. School District U-46 embarked upon a comprehensive redesign to adhere to best practices in gifted education with an acute focus on equity and excellence. An unlikely opportunity created by a lawsuit changed the scope of the district's perspective on what it meant to adequately identify and serve diverse gifted learners. The core of the redesign was aimed at creating equity-centered, sustainable programming that highlighted opportunities for all high-ability learners. We (the educators and stakeholders in my district, and I) unapologetically used the required reporting to move in the direction of expanding access to underrepresented students. The goal of equitable gifted programs centered on access, representation, meaningful participation, and high outcomes for students, regardless of race, dominant language, or socioeconomic status. This clarion call signaled a need for change, and we were up for the arduous, but necessary, task.

Background

Gifted programs have been in District U-46 for more than 40 years. In adherence to the district mission, *all* means all. The district is committed to improving the academic achievement of *all* gifted students. Much of the redesign was facilitated using the guiding principles of the NAGC (2010) Pre-K–Grade 12 Gifted Programming Standards. Our efforts reflect evidenced-based educational best practices for gifted students to succeed.

In 2004, the district faced a discrimination lawsuit. Although the lawsuit has become notoriously recognized because of gifted education, the initial impetus for the lawsuit did not originate with gifted programming. The lawsuit, filed by five Black and Latino families, was prompted by U-46 changing school boundaries in 2004 and concentrating students in neighborhood schools. The lawsuit itself came on the heels of No Child Left Behind (2001), in which there was a push for English proficiency. From the boundary changes and people feeling that students were being exited prematurely from English language services, the lawsuit emerged. The charge was threefold:

1. the system purposely discriminated against a specific race and ethnicity,
2. the system purposely discriminated against students for special education services, and
3. the district specifically discriminated against Black and Latino students in advanced placement and gifted services.

As the lawsuit progressed, questions around gifted education surfaced. Underrepresentation refers to the disproportionate number of students in gifted programs as it relates to a group's overall representation in the school's or district's population. The representation indices for Black and Latino students were staggering. U-46 is a large school district that serves 40,000 students in 57 schools and programs—five high schools, eight middle schools, 40 elementary schools, two early childhood learning centers, and two alternative schools. The district's population at the time of the lawsuit was about 50% Hispanic, 30% White, 6%–7% African American, and 9% Asian. The demographics have been pretty stable, except that the Latino population has continued to grow, and the White population has continued to decline.

At the time of the lawsuit, around 20% of our students were English language learners (ELLs) and 51% were from impoverished backgrounds. These dynamics point to opportunities that represent challenges faced by urban districts throughout the nation. The students in gifted programming did not adequately represent the cultural and linguistic diversity of students in the district, except in one of our programs in which we had a large Latino population. The

SET SWAS (Spanish English Transitional School Within a School) program had the largest concentration of Latino students in gifted programming.

> *Underrepresentation refers to the disproportionate number of students in gifted programs as it relates to a group's overall representation in the school's or district's population.*

Within the SET SWAS program, bilingual, gifted, Spanish-dominant students in grades 4, 5, and 6 received instruction at specific sites. The program included instruction in which content, pacing, and depth were commensurate with student ability. The overall goals and objectives corresponded with the SWAS (monolingual gifted) curriculum. In addition, students were given the opportunity to communicate across all domains (speaking, listening, writing, and reading) in both English and Spanish in an effort to foster and nurture bilingualism. Students were grouped homogeneously as identified by a cadre of assessments, including interviews. The program was created based on the idea that gifted English language learners benefited from specialized instructional programming to service both their bilingualism and giftedness in an instructional setting. We determined that the students were continuing to acquire English as an additional language; thus, they needed specialized support to nurture their giftedness while bridging language barriers. The environment we structured was intended to meet the unique academic and social-emotional needs of bilingual gifted learners.

Teachers supported students throughout the program and any transitions. Students could transition into the English gifted classes at the elementary level, or they could choose to maintain their participation in SET SWAS for all of elementary school. At the middle school level there was only SWAS, a monolingual gifted program.

All students, those from SWAS and SET SWAS, attended the same middle school program. All instruction for middle school gifted students was in English.

The identification and delivery models for SET SWAS were determined as a part of the district's plan for facilitating representative support for language minority students, allowing them to develop their native language and English as an additional language, while having gifted services to meet their intellectual needs. This delivery model for bilingual services was aligned with the requirements of Illinois State Board of Education Bilingual Program.

As part of meeting the needs of students in the federally funded and state-funded bilingual programs, the district designated English language learning centers, under the English Language Learners Department, that were spread out in the community. Students were bused to campuses as a district-agreed way to provide services. Although the intent was to bring students back to their neighborhood schools after students' time at the designated English language learning centers, we ran into the unintended consequence of segregating the district. That alerted the parents who contacted a law firm. This particular law firm specialized in class action lawsuits related to whether an organization has specifically segregated or harmed students. The law firm had a record of suing districts and creating consent decrees. In those instances, districts would go ahead and agree without admitting guilt, and they would complete some remediation. That remediation always included some kind of consent decree that was constructed by lawyers and had to be monitored. District U-46, at the time, decided to fight the lawsuit. The law firm won on one of the three counts—one of our programs was found to be discriminatory. The judge determined that SET SWAS discriminated against students based on ethnicity because only Spanish-speaking students were in SET SWAS. The directive behind SET SWAS was to provide programming that would meet the needs of those students while fostering bilingualism and biliteracy within an environment conducive to their needs. It was never to discriminate against students.

The Road to Redesign

The 9-year-old discrimination lawsuit against the district was settled in 2013. The school board unanimously approved the $2.5 million settlement agreement in the case of *McFadden v. Board of Education for Illinois School District U-46.* The judge determined that the school district discriminated against Latino students by placing them in a separate, segregated elementary gifted program. He called for us to fix issues with the gifted program. The gifted agreement required that the district would fix the issues by the beginning of the 2014–2015 school year. Even before the settlement agreement was reached, the district developed a revised and expanded elementary program for gifted students. As part of our commitment and investment in shifting gears in the overhaul, we put corrective actions in place in areas we identified. Per the agreement, we submitted two reports to the court, in August 2015 and August 2016, about the implementation of the gifted program. Both of the reports satisfied the judge's desired implementation.

Beyond merely reporting the improvements to the court, we endeavored to redesign the program so it reflected best practices in gifted education. We wanted to not only remedy issues and address the specifics that came under review during the lawsuit, but also improve the program. We recognized that the revisions were long overdue. We endeavored to come out of this precarious situation better, and also expand the program to improve student experiences. Early intervention is key, and we determined that, by increasing and offering programming at lower grades, we would work to close the opportunity gap.

Our delivery model and teacher preparation were central items we considered as we embarked upon the redesign. Ensuring that all students, regardless of language background, had sufficient resources in accessing the gifted curriculum, we implemented mandatory endorsement requirements for all teachers. Any teachers who taught in the gifted program at the elementary level had to complete their English as a second language (ESL) endorsement.

To amply serve students from Spanish-speaking homes, our system recognized that all teachers must have the requisite coursework and training that prepares them to meet the needs of second-language learners. This was necessary not only for emergent bilingual students, but also for students who were bilingual refusals. Having a bilingual endorsed educator ensured that appropriate instructional strategies reflected second-language acquisition, thus elevating the status of a child's native language.

> *We were zealous in providing pathways for students who were traditionally overlooked in the district.*

We used the redesign to move toward our equity goals. Another way we advanced the equity work within gifted programming was by making improvements that included implementing a talent development program. We were zealous in providing pathways for students who were traditionally overlooked in the district. We moved forward with a program that included talent spotting. This was hard to pull off in the context of the hard financial situation we were in; the absence of funding and gifted mandate from the state did not help. We used what we had, and that was the findings from the discrimination lawsuit. Equity in gifted education became a new priority. We used the crisis to improve programming. As the gifted specialist, I worked with our external gifted expert on the redesign, including an emphasis on the talent development program for students in grades 1–3.

My motivation for my involvement in the redesign was twofold: I am a product of the district, and it is where I started my career in education. It was befitting that I returned to the district to facilitate the redesign. I grew up as a child of poverty and had first-hand knowledge of the power and access made available through advocacy. I was overlooked for gifted services until middle school. Through support from cultural brokers, I advocated for placement change and was subsequently placed in the appropriate classes that matched my ability and set forth a trajectory that mirrored my scholarly disposition. I utilized my capacity and propensity to take purposeful initiative. Discovering more about my talents and ability, I sought meaning and produced the changes in my academic career that I desired in my life. Gifted education represents a delicately balanced union of my personal and professional pursuits.

When we looked at U-46 gifted services, not only were we charged with redesigning programming, but also we had a chance to get it right. We were presented with an opportunity to align our local programming standards to those set forth by NAGC (2010). The redesign of the district philosophy and mission articulated the importance of providing gifted education services to students from diverse backgrounds, and included belief statements, goals, and objectives that were evident in our practices. We were able to combine our understandings of equity and excellence, specifically within the work of gifted education. This was a place where I was interested in involving myself in the fight for equity in gifted education for underserved learners who come from marginalized backgrounds.

The Redesigned Gifted Programming

District U-46 now has the IGNITE (Inquiry and Gifted Network for Ingenuity and Talent Exploration) program. Throughout the redesign, we had the benefit of looking at our values and beliefs and how they inform everything from teacher selection, to student recruitment, parent advisory, and all facets of gifted programming. The timing was right for us to engage in a comprehensive redesign of programming so that we could provide a level of programming that would maximize student educational outcomes. This positioned us to move to a strengths-based approach, specifically in how we viewed students from diverse backgrounds. This shift was instrumental in allowing our sidelined talent to take off, thus taking our students to levels of programming that we knew would be possible in gifted education.

Our initial steps involved work in areas that caused us to calibrate our mindset. Our new work represented a departure from antiquated standards of giftedness that resided at the intersection of privilege and elitism. We started by looking at our definition of giftedness. We oriented ourselves around the work by identifying who we were talking about, exactly who would be considered gifted in District U-46. Giftedness, in most instances, is locally defined, and programming should be set forth using local criteria, in addition to adherence to state regulations in order to identify and serve students where gifted programming is implemented. We had an opportunity to use language that would honor equity in gifted education. We understood that there may be barriers, cultural conflicts, or other factors that might preclude a student's identification for gifted programming. Those barriers could be attributed to previous learning opportunities, lived experiences, language, or poverty. We recognized that leveling the playing field was essential to achieve adequate representation.

We recognized that leveling the playing field was essential to achieve adequate representation.

We decided to utilize a more encompassing definition of giftedness and take an opportunity to look more holistically at students in our schools. Gifted students are those who perform, or show the potential to perform, at remarkably high levels of accomplishment when compared with students of their comparable age, experience, and/or environment. Gifted students exhibit high performance capacity and general intellectual ability or ability in a specific academic field. A major gamechanger in the definition of giftedness within District U-46 is the language that diversifies giftedness. We embrace that gifted students are found in *all* ethnic or socioeconomic groups and that they require specialized instruction services and/or activities that are not ordinarily provided by the general education program in order to maximize the academic and social and emotional pursuits of high-ability learners.

Barriers to rigorous programming include English as an additional language, poverty, cultural bias, access to enrichment, policies, and procedures. In order to assess for underrepresentation in a school or district, the following questions must be posed:

1. Are students from all demographic populations represented in the assessment, nomination, identification, and exit within gifted programs?
2. Where are the discrepancies occurring?

The new definition of giftedness permitted us to cast a wider net in order to provide adequate services. By looking at more students from throughout the district, we were able to see the varied manifestations of ability at our local level. We were not comfortable with what the demographics of our former program suggested about our overall population. Everything we put toward our new philosophy yielded productive programming for all of our students in our continuum of services—from the time students first enter AIM (Access to Inquiry and Meaning), our talent development program.

> *Gifted students are those who perform, or show the potential to perform, at remarkably high levels of accomplishment when compared with students of their comparable age, experience, and/or environment.*

Talent spotting is a gamechanger, providing students with an occasion to showcase their potential in a nonthreatening environment in which emphasis is placed on the rigor of students' thinking skills. Inevitably, the skills nurtured in talent development are transferred to content area instruction, thus permitting students to engage more fully in core academics. Talent development is now delivered in second and third grade, with the hope that we can eventually implement talent development as early as possible. As with other areas of intervention, talent development yields the most effective response when students experience the intervention at the early grades.

Our philosophy is from a district perspective that orients all facets of our programming in accordance with our district strategic plan. The way we operationalize our understanding of giftedness has become a more essential function of our system. Through consulting with colleagues and experts on the state and national level, we greatly considered how to orient our district expectations around what giftedness would look like. Our program needed to have our fingerprints on it because we have immeasurable skin in the game in serving our learners. We have committed to not only recognizing our need, but also meeting it. Giftedness is an integral function of our system. We operate in alignment with the values we have set forth, and we embrace that our district gifted program should reflect the rich linguistic, racial, and socioeconomic diversity in our district.

In response to advocacy work happening under the Illinois Association for Gifted Children (IAGC), we wanted our efforts in redesigning our gifted identification policy at the local level to embrace a widely held understanding of equitable identification protocol. Our district policy was developed in response to changes prompted by the tireless advocacy and collaboration of IAGC and other organizations. Looking through an equity lens, we modified the district's identification and placement process to provide consistency, fairness, and inclusive practices of students across racial and socioeconomic demographics. We looked at the definition of giftedness based on the work that was facilitated by IAGC. We were not only looking for those students who perform or have demonstrated achievement, but also recognizing students who have potential and deserve an opportunity for programming. Potential does not always manifest in ways that educators identify; those manifestations may be impacted by language differences, previous opportunities for learning, or inputs from culture and/or lived experiences. In the spirit of honoring diversity and inclusion, we are able to scrutinize our program and tailor it to the exact needs of the students we serve. We endeavor to uphold and honor the integrity of our philosophy in all that we do in gifted education.

> *We embrace that our program should reflect the rich ethnic, linguistic, and socioeconomic diversity of our district.*

It is interesting to see the way we operationalize our understanding of the gifted. To effectively implement our definition of giftedness, it had to become a function of our system and had to be part of the fabric of our district. We embrace that our program should reflect the ethnic, linguistic, and socioeconomic diversity of our district. We have the luxury of having a widely diverse district, and it would be the equivalent of education malpractice to have a gifted program that does not look like the students we serve. When looking through a strengths-based model, we are able to talent spot and find all gifted students. They are in our district. These students are bright; we had to adjust so we recognized their skills for exactly what they are. We acknowledge there is a need not only for intellectually engaging stimulation, but also for a place where innovation and exploration are honored.

Additional New Programming Considerations

In writing the agreement that we brought to the court, we considered the multifaceted approach that was necessary to develop and sustain a gifted model that represented best practices, as well as aligned with our district vision and goals. The agreement was driven by us, in that it was developed by us and implemented by us, and we are held accountable for it. The plaintiff did not drive the agreement. The result is an understanding and realization of best practices that we embraced as we redesigned our programming. It was incumbent upon us to do something. We consulted and considered a broad range of ideas that would allow us to leave the gifted education program and the district better than we found it. We realized that we had to do something, and we needed something that would be sustainable—something we would be accountable for that would have immediate impact on the students from groups that had previously not been allowed access to gifted programs in District U-46. To demonstrate our endeavors to make things right, we structured a gifted charter and internal team with varying stakeholders, consisting of district administrators from various departments, including our English Language Learners Department, specialized student services, and legal department. We had intentionally focused on various places in the district to assist with the development of our program. Equitable gifted education was a goal for our administrative team.

Some of the structures that have been changed since the redesign are ones that could have been changed organically. Such magnitude of changes would have involved bringing groups together to embark upon a thorough review, which could have been done with internal and external experts. The fact that we wrote the agreement, presented it to the court, and said what we would like to be accountable for allowed us to drive the process. We had keen insight into our program's deficiencies. We discovered that much of what we implemented through the redesign was simply an adherence to best practices in specialized programming. The level of engagement from district-level administrators throughout the redesign was notable. We ensured that there was equity by allowing voice and representation from individuals who have a thorough understanding of equitable access and excellence in education.

Through the thoughtful leadership of our former superintendent, I facilitated the redesign in collaboration with various district administrators. In a matter of weeks, we determined that universal screening was the most efficient method for access to the identification process. We collaborated extensively with our vendor to procure the necessary testing materials, professional development for staff, and training for test proctors. In a district with 40 elementary buildings, we were able to implement a test schedule, provide notification to parents and all teachers, and host assessment overviews, along with our gifted overview, for all parents with students in each affected grade level. Considering the scope of our district, it was necessary to offer the overviews on multiple nights and at various times to capture the widest audience to communicate this notable change for gifted services. A clear part of our redesign focuses on outreach tailored at remedying underrepresented and untapped potential. Our number one goal was to make things right, to make gifted programming in school District U-46 reflect equity and access, which ultimately yields excellence in education.

> *Our number one goal was to make things right, to make gifted programming in school District U-46 reflect equity and access, which ultimately yields excellence in education.*

Although our efforts to provide equitable access have been admirable, they have not been without resistance. We recognized there was significant learning that needed to take place for all stakeholders to understand our redesign and its goals. In some instances, much of the targeted professional development has been aimed at meeting the needs of the teachers of gifted. Not unique to school District U-46, gifted education has some components that foster elitism. There is an idea or belief that gifted students always get the correct answers and show up on time with their things—neat, organized, and prepared to do school. This is according to a prescribed set of values that are oriented around a middle-class, predominantly White system in public education. Part of our program review involved analyzing our district data for an understanding of those who served as teachers of gifted. We needed to recognize the potential cultural conflicts for teachers serving students who did not look like them or did not come from similar backgrounds.

The assessment instruments we use for gifted screening are the Cognitive Abilities Test (CogAT), Measures of Academic Progress (MAP), and an observation checklist, the Teacher Inventory of Learning Strengths (TILS). We triangulate the data from these three inputs in order to develop more comprehensive student profiles. No single piece is used as the sole determinant for a student getting in or being excluded from programming. No portion of the identification process has a weight or value assigned to it. We previously used the Naglieri Nonverbal Ability Test (NNAT-2) with our students in SET SWAS. There are implied thoughts and beliefs around the NNAT-2 and the use of other nonverbal assessments as ways to increase the population of diverse students in gifted programs. We understood that we were measuring the same abilities across various student groups, and obviously, because of students coming from different backgrounds, the data would look different. As pointed out in research, the use of the nonverbal instrument was not the way for us to attain equitable identification. Such instruments are considered culturally neutral and therefore better for gifted identification, but they should not be the sole instrument for gifted screening of students from diverse backgrounds (NAGC, n.d.-a). Consideration must also be given to how an instrument's measures reflect the program students are being considered for. The answer is rarely as simple as which test to administer.

The way to make sense of the differences was to use local norms when identifying for gifted programming. Again, with 40 elementary buildings in a district that covers 11 communities with varied demographics across all of the areas, developing a single identification strand that adequately represents the needs, strengths, and abilities of all students in the district is difficult. With a system designed around neighborhood schools, students generally attend schools with classmates who have comparable backgrounds and similar experiences. Comparing students to peers from comparable backgrounds just makes sense. We do not need to further stratify student abilities by comparing students from some of our neighborhood schools that are in areas that happen to be more economically vulnerable to students from schools in the neighborhood where there is more affluence and social capital.

In District U-46, we use one measure to identify all students regardless of dominant language, and the bold step we have taken is to analyze the data and have in-depth conversations about what the data suggest. Inequity can manifest with the use of any instrument. Nonverbal tests are not the panacea. The search for the perfect instrument is an exercise in futility. Considering that children come from different backgrounds and have different experiences afforded or withheld from them foreshadows the inequities educators can see in academic achievement. To truly address the issue, the differences in educational opportunity must be addressed. Thus, we do not compare students from low-income backgrounds to their higher income counterparts. Looking at students from impoverished backgrounds and comparing them to students who are non-low poverty is ineffective and wrong. Doing so only displays the impact of the differences in educational opportunities. The differences (e.g., where students live, what experiences they are exposed to, etc.) are not indicators of their ability. Comparing students to peers of comparable backgrounds gives insight into what students are capable of. We can assess their strengths relative to previous opportunities for learning. Poverty is insidious. Our scholars, however, are not poor. They come with a wealth of experiences, thinking skills, and opportunities that will permit them to learn and make significant gains when in educational environments that honor their strengths. Using local norms to leverage participation in programming has had a gamechanging impact.

In order to reach the untapped potential of students who are from underserved backgrounds, educators must first identify these students, and then serve them. Developing critical mass is a central feature of identifying and retaining students from underserved backgrounds. Students from diverse backgrounds may have to negotiate a balance, in which they learn to embrace the intersectionality of their identities. Being a minority in a learning environment in which the majority of peers are White or Asian may cause Black and Latino students to experience stereotype threat.

Diverse students may believe that they are the representatives for their whole group and that their performance will be construed as representation for the whole group. All students deserve to learn in environments in which they see themselves as capable. In District U-46, we have been able to foster this critical mass by implementing a talent development program. Frontloading experiences (i.e., providing enriched learning experiences for all students before identifying for gifted students) provides systemic talent development that allows all students access to learning environments before we screen for gifted students. Part of our professional development plan requires that all teachers and administrators complete training in the gifted education seminar (GES). The GES is provided through the partnership of IAGC and the Illinois State Board of Education (ISBE). With the GES, we are able to develop foundational understanding that is consistent throughout the district. From the initial foundational exposure, there are planned professional learning experiences in gifted education throughout the year.

Beyond gifted screening in our district, at the elementary level in grades 4–6, once identified as gifted, a student is permitted to keep that label and remain in gifted programming from elementary through middle school. That may sound uncomplicated, but when you are reviewing your district parameters around equity participation and retention for students who come from marginalized backgrounds, it is important. Simply recruiting, identifying, and using universal screening is not enough. Once identified, students need to understand that they will be able to matriculate through the gifted offerings without disruption to their participation in the program. We decided to no longer "ungift" students. We address that in District U-46 by allowing students to keep their label. Although we do not "ungift" students, we do recognize that there can be scenarios and situations in which students face difficulty navigating through the gifted program, but our desire is to engage in a thought-provoking problem-solving approach to identify the root causes of either the underachievement, lack of engagement, or whatever other cause may be identified. We have implemented an exit procedure. The safety clause in the exit procedure requires us to explore who is exited from the program and under what conditions an exit may be necessary. Central to the work in the exit procedure is the collaborative nature of the decision making, which must include parents, teachers, the principal, and the gifted coordinator. We found that we had a disproportionate number of students exiting or students being helped to leave gifted programming as they transitioned through different program levels.

> *Cultural brokering is meeting students at critical points, providing access and opportunities.*

We recognize that students from diverse backgrounds—either linguistically, racially or ethnically, or socioeconomically—may experience stereotype threat or other psychosocial experiences that impact the way they engage in programming. Since uncovering such instances, we have developed supports and interventions aimed at helping students to see themselves in their true capacity as they operate in the gifted environment. This level of work is one that I consider cultural brokering. Cultural brokering is meeting students at critical points and providing access and opportunities. This brokering includes determining which tools and resources should be made readily available to permit students to engage in programming without restraint due to extraneous variables. Cultural brokering is similar to a scaffold, providing support for students until they are able to do something independently.

Although there are always additional strides to make, our program is functioning at an acceptable level for what we have at this time. The court proceedings allowed us to develop practices so that we could remedy the identified issues. However, all of what became our operating procedures was not necessarily supported. We recognize that our current programming works when people of goodwill are ruling, but in the absence of those advocates, programming of this level of specificity will not be sustained. To honor the perpetuity of our redesign, we have to get the practices codified as Board of Education policy. We are continuing to make progress, and the district is working toward institutionalizing our procedures as part of board policy. All of our procedures that were changed as a result of the lawsuit have been escalated to the Board of Education.

REFLECTION QUESTIONS

1. In what ways is your gifted implementation similar to that of District U-46?

2. Identify three ways your current identification protocol perpetuates underrepresentation.

3. How do you anticipate engaging in bold conversations in gifted education when issues of race, language, and SES are involved?

4. What changes could be made to make your gifted screening more equitable?

5. What steps can you take to raise awareness about disproportionality in your gifted program?

CHAPTER 3

Identification

Most conversations about gifted education include hardy discussion around the identification and selection of students. Fraught with challenges, identification systems can pose unintended consequences. The procedures for selecting which students gain access to gifted education can vary extensively. Local education agencies follow their state guidelines, and in the absence of such legislation, identification is carried out following parameters established at the local level.

Gifted identification should be viewed as a way to respond to the need for instructional settings that succinctly meet students' needs. Advanced academic programs, as extensions of the core general education program, can also provide pathways to differentiated educational programming for high-potential students. Beginning identification processes early in students' school careers provides ample opportunity to provide intervention and enrichment, which are critical for addressing underrepresentation. Additionally, ensuring ongoing identification—with equal access, universal screening, or universal consideration—increases the number of students who are served in gifted education. Providing multiple opportunities across students' educational careers to participate in universal screening is key in ongoing identification.

A challenge District U-46 has fought to disassociate from is the use of arbitrary cutoffs, national norms, general gifted characteristics, and teacher referral or nomination. National norms reflect what is perceived to be the standard. National norm comparisons yield different numbers of students identified for gifted services with an emphasis placed on students from more affluent backgrounds. Although the use of national norms purports a level of fairness and consistency, it actually produces bias against students from certain groups or benefits students from higher socioeconomics. As a district, we have sought to implement processes in which students with similar experiences, backgrounds, and environments are compared, so that we deliver services to the brightest students from all of our buildings, instead of the brightest students in the district. A way to approach integral gifted programming reflective of equitable practices is to stop using national norms for identifying for local programs. When used as a deciding factor, national norms severely constrain the candidate pool. The correlation between achievement and income highlights one of the most prolific sources of inequitable educational outcomes.

Implementing Universal Screening

Universal screening is a way to optimize policies for identifying students. Universal screening, or universal consideration, has been shown to increase the representation indices for underrepresented minority students, as well as students from economically vulnerable households (Lakin, 2016). Universal screening casts a wider net, increasing the proportion of historically underrepresented students in gifted education programs. Districts must consider the type of instrument they select for their assessment. It is critical that the tool be linked to the level of services offered through the gifted program. By removing barriers to the identification pool, access is widened.

In District U-46, we administer the gifted screening as a universal screening, which is the systematic testing of all students at a grade level. Universal screening measures students' ability and potential, unlike traditional assessments, which only measure achievement. Achievement tests cannot be used as universal screeners. The universal screening process is a critical part of the gifted and talented identification process. Universal screening allows a greater number of students to be considered for gifted and talented identification, particularly those from traditionally underrepresented populations, such as minority students, English language learners, and students living at the poverty level. Universal screening provides a big picture review of the data for the cohort, which helps compose a talent pool. Universal screening allows for detailed data analysis, specifically through the use of local norms.

We created wider access to our candidate pool by removing the barrier of having to be invited to test for the gifted program, as our former system required. We like to think of the screening as universal consideration for all students to enter the identification pool. Since implementing universal screening in 2012/2013, we have found a more diverse candidate pool. Universal screening alone is not enough to meet the necessary metrics for equitable programming. As previously noted, in addition to universal screening, we have implemented the use of local normative criteria to identify students for gifted programming. The use of local norms permits us to develop and analyze the data of the students currently sitting in the classrooms of District U-46.

No single instrument is going to be the answer to underrepresentation.

By using local building-level norms (i.e., ranked performance within the school), we are able to identify overlooked gems, and we can more adeptly resolve disproportionality rates that we have experienced along racial lines. A local norms approach is more aligned with the goal of gifted education. The use of local normative criteria increases participation in gifted programming by students from traditionally underserved populations. We have made significant strides in identifying students who have not been traditionally identified for gifted programming. Realizing that gifted identification disparities occur alongside excellence gaps points out how much restrictive practices, such as the reliance on inordinately high performance levels on assessments matched to national norms, contribute to disproportionality rates.

Considering that achievement gaps among subgroups of students performing at the highest levels of achievement exist, attention is brought to improving schools and communities, which results in maximizing potential among the fastest growing populations. But the types of interventions that must be implemented to close excellence gaps can vary (Plucker & Peters, 2018). With the use of local norms, for example, identifying students (from our 40 elementary buildings) who are within the top 5%–7% (varies by cohort annually) has significantly impacted the diversity of our district program. The use of local norms is an articulated way to yield more responsive participation in gifted programming for students from diverse populations. Through the use of identification by local norms, students are more likely to be compared to peers who are from similar backgrounds. The heavy conversations around test bias and the like are futile and do not get the field closer to identifying students from marginalized backgrounds. No single instrument is going to be the answer to underrepresentation. The country's educational system is flawed. While educators wait for a complete overhaul in the public education services that are delivered, districts can make changes in gifted education by modifying the elements that are under their control.

Dismantling Screening Barriers

Identification is a targeted approach we consider in our process of responsive identification in District U-46. All students at a grade level for universal screening (in our case, third and sixth grade) participate in the screening, achievement, and ability instruments that are part of the gifted identification and selection process. Prior to the district's redesign, students had to be invited to test for gifted programming. The threshold for an invitation for testing was set at an inordinate level: Students had to score at the 92nd percentile or higher on an achievement test in order to be invited to take the Cognitive Abilities Test. In addition to the high threshold, students had to test on a Saturday morning, in many instances traveling from elementary school neighborhoods where public transportation was not readily available or accessible. For students from economically vulnerable households, transportation can pose a significant barrier, and we decided to dismantle that barrier and provide access by offering the gifted screening during the school day.

We also recognized that achievement as a universal screener is not plausible because of all of the extraneous variables that go into an achievement measure. We decided to look beyond demonstrated achievement and spot for areas that gave us insight into what students would be able to do with the appropriate level of supports. The former model served as a gatekeeping structure for gifted services. The exclusivity of our program was in direct opposition to our district's strategic plan. Our district vision is "academic success for all," and *all* means all, but that same consideration was not extended to students from diverse populations with respect to accessing gifted programs.

We use terms like *responsive identification* because we recognized that there were some areas that we needed to remedy or bring to a resolution. The historical underrepresentation by students who were Black or Latino, or who qualified for free or reduced meals, was staggering. When we implemented the universal screening in the 2012–2013 school year, we started screening at third grade. Our gifted program starts at fourth grade. Moving away from national norms and an invitation or referral process has allowed us to provide programming that reflects our students. In systems where a referral is part of the gifted identification, parental advocacy is an initial factor for identification, and some groups have more social capital in order to navigate such structures. For groups that do not have the similar level of social capital or navigational capital, their opportunities to gain access to programs through a nomination or referral base is significantly lower. Families from both of the backgrounds have similar care for, compassion for, and belief in their children. The difference is access because of a family's social capital. In District U-46, we have programming that is developed locally with the needs of our students, community, and stakeholders in mind. We moved away from the practice of using achievement measures or a referral process in favor of universal screening to honor the untapped potential we knew our learners possessed.

More Lessons From District U-46

We identified that we had a disproportionate number of students from underrepresented backgrounds exiting or being helped to leave gifted programming as they transitioned to middle school. We no longer require testing for placement during transition periods. As previously noted, students who are identified gifted in elementary continue through gifted programming in middle school. From an equity perspective, we had to ensure that all students were provided adequate levels of support to continue in the program. In years to come, following the changes in District U-46, IAGC collaborated with other organizations and advocates to propose legislation requiring districts to report on the numbers of students exiting gifted programs or services by demographics. This is instrumental in ascertaining the retention rate of gifted students from diverse populations.

We want to avoid any single measure determining a child's placement.

In addition to the use of local building-level criteria, we have checklists as part of the identification protocol. Teachers, parents, and administrators receive training on the instrument and its use in gifted identification. The training is layered with work from our district equity plan; teachers are encouraged to complete profiles. The use of multiple measures helps us gain a wider view of the students. We want to avoid any single measure determining a child's placement. Since using local norms, we have found that our identification cohorts are a closer representation of the district demographics.

Our IGNITE program at the elementary level is from fourth through sixth grade, and gifted programming is hosted at nine of our elementary buildings. Students are assigned a gifted site based on feeder patterns at the elementary level. In addition to feeder patterns, we strive to achieve balanced representation at gifted sites for students based on socioeconomic status (as determined by participation in the free and reduced meals program) and ethnicity, as well as language status. This permits us to develop programming sites with balanced representation that more accurately reflects the district's demographics. We certainly want to ensure that we are not further segregating students and instead developing sites that include a majority of minority students, ELLs, or low-income learners. Permitting students to interact with diverse groups of learners benefits all learners.

In addition to our English program, we offer a dual language IGNITE program, which fosters the biliteracy, bilingualism, and biculturalism for students from Spanish-dominant homes, as well as homes with other native languages. Dual language IGNITE programming is for students who have participated in dual language programming from kindergarten or first grade in the district. IGNITE and dual language IGNITE have the same overarching framework. The difference is noted in language for instruction. The mixing of cultural and social capital in the dual language IGNITE program is a deliberate attempt to permit students to engage in authentic learning experiences that provide scaffolds for them to interact globally as global citizens. This effort was a collaborative undertaking that involved working with transportation, our facilities, and our enrollment in order to maximize program participation at all sites. Our dual language IGNITE program is a 50-50 language allocation by third grade, so when students start IGNITE at fourth grade, you cannot readily identify a student's language background. We strive for balanced bilingual students, and we have demonstrated through qualitative as well as quantitative data that students are making sufficient growth.

REFLECTION QUESTIONS

1. Educators need to do things differently in order to see different results. How can you advocate so policies catch up with that notion?

2. How do teacher nominations perpetuate disproportionality across racial and ethnic lines?

3. How will you respond to pushback about the use of local norms from stakeholders who are more accustomed to using national norms?

CHAPTER 4

Talent Spotting

Raising awareness about what privilege looks like in gifted programming involves heavy lifting. National norm comparisons for gifted identification have been widely used for years. Addressing the inequities that arise from such restrictive identification protocols has proven to be difficult. Educators, parents, and stakeholders who hold longstanding perceptions of giftedness and notions of exceptionality may be reluctant to respond to the inequities and cast wider nets for gifted identification. In a field that has historically and overwhelmingly identified White and Asian students for services, equitable identification has been criticized for permitting "unqualified" students to access programming. At the same time, the field at large recognizes the constraints of gifted programs, namely with regard to identification and the unequal results it yields, but there has not been clear focus on ways to remedy underrepresentation.

The notion of exceptionality has historically been associated with Whiteness and middle-class values. Raising awareness about underrepresentation is only the beginning. Challenges abound with implementations aimed at addressing underrepresentation and creating responsive practices that will yield sustainable participation by students from diverse populations. Although disproportionality (i.e., inequities in participation in gifted programs by students from diverse populations) is easy to identify, sustainable strategies aimed at making strides in responsive participation can be challenging to implement. This shift allows educators to tap potential of students who are overwhelming excluded from programs for high-ability learners. Although 2014 was the first year that schools were majority minority, gifted programs have not evolved to reflect the population shift. For example, according to national statistics, in the 2013–2014 school year, Black (15.5%) and Latino (24.8%) students made up 40.3% of the public school population, but they only made up 28% of students in gifted programs (U.S. Department of Education, Office for Civil Rights, 2014). Emergent bilinguals or ELLs were the most disproportionately represented groups.

> *Talent development not only is a potential pathway to gifted services, but also may be a way to close the excellence gap.*

Elitist gifted programs assess students' privilege. With an understanding of the power of language and an awareness of culture, the intersectionality of identity is foundational in talent development programs. For years, educators have identified students and then served them; talent development flips that model. Students are provided exposure to enrichment as a platform for their talents to emerge and be nurtured. Talent development is a way to level the playing field for students who have not had similar previous opportunities for learning when compared to those of their more affluent peers. Talent development can be a service in the continuum of services, acting as one delivery model in the umbrella of gifted services. Talent development not only is a potential pathway to gifted services, but also may be a way to close the excellence gap. The excellence gap measures the disproportionate participation rates of low-income students in advanced learning environments as well as the unequal outcomes of students from low-income households at advanced levels. The gap appears before students enroll in elementary school and continues as students matriculate through middle school, high school, college, and beyond.

As the number of minority students increases and income disparity in the U.S. grows, educators must address excellence gaps in student achievement. Untapped potential is costly and has far-reaching consequences. The nation cannot flourish if children from all racial and economic groups do not maximize their full potential. Closing excellence gaps is not just about more research on how to remove barriers and creating a climate in which all children can succeed at the highest levels; it is about building a foundation of seeing diverse gifted learners and serving them. There is much educators already know, and this knowledge must be represented in practices and policies.

Talent Development in District U-46

Talent development takes place in grades 2–3 in all of the 24 Title I schools in District U-46. We have 10 gifted specialists who serve in AIM talent development. We microtarget our Title I schools, schools with the highest incidences of underrepresented populations by grade level. We target equity as we talent spot. Providing gifted education as enrichment is an intervention that invites students from historically underrepresented backgrounds to access experiences and environments that will be instrumental in tapping their potential and maximizing their trajectories (Olszewski-Kubilius & Clarenbach, 2012; Plucker & Peters, 2016; Worrell, 2010). Yes, some students have gaps and skills that need to be remedied, but we fundamentally believe that all students should have access to enrichment. It is possible to provide both enrichment and core service to students who have some gaps in their demonstrated achievement and are not meeting grade-level standards. We work to identify potential in students. Then, we turn that potential into talent.

Scholars see a gifted specialist on a weekly basis. Each gifted specialist pushes into a class for 45 minutes of targeted thinking skills instruction. The expectation is that the classroom teacher observes students. The classroom teacher collects data on how students respond to the intervention. The classroom teacher and gifted specialist combine their thoughts and ideas about students and students' experiences in the areas of thinking (evaluative, visual, convergent, and divergent). Classroom teachers are encouraged to participate in training, which gives them insight into the types of behaviors we are looking for as students experience an intervention. Educators have shared how seeing their students engage in learning during AIM has opened their eyes to students' abilities. Educators have realized students' untapped skills. Each lesson includes multiple stages in the learning process, including modeled, shared, guided, and independent practice. There is also a reflection piece tied into the lesson. We teach students how to tap their critical and creative thinking skills to their fullest potential.

A big piece of programming is providing the necessary scaffolding for students to access the curriculum. It is great that we are permitted to teach these thinking skills without the heaviness of content. All students are able to think. Having the chance to see how students think and explain their reasoning allows us to assess students' potential and their ability to function in a gifted setting with the appropriate level of support and balanced expectations. Each lesson has strands from literacy and/or math, plus social-emotional learning standards. The literacy and math standards are outlined in the Common Core State Standards (CCSS). Students are using higher vocabulary that corresponds with the levels of thinking. Each teacher understands that she is bringing a certain amount of capital in access to the playing field and has made a commitment to fostering an environment in which students can succeed at high levels.

We teach students how to tap their skills in thinking critically and creatively to their fullest potential.

Part of this instruction is the deliberate focus on academic vocabulary. AIM presents a "just right" challenge for students. Every student is given the opportunity to succeed. The skills students learn with their gifted specialist directly transfer to the skills that are necessary in the core academic areas. Gifted specialists are expected to go into classrooms and elevate the level of language in a way that makes it part of students' toolkits. Programming itself is not the pathway. Part of the remedy to underrepresentation hinges on the access and resources that are provided, and as cultural brokers, we provide experiences that promote greater access for students. Gifted specialists are advocates for the students they service. They compile academic behavioral portfolios to use during the identification and selection committee work. Gifted specialists engage with the students for this yearlong program; in many instances, the gifted specialist is able to loop with the students (i.e., teach the same group of students at second and third grade).

A critical element of encouraging potential that has been underutilized is developing rapport with an adult throughout educational pursuits. The gifted specialists operate in this capacity. The talent development process (i.e., providing access to students and talent spotting) builds a pipeline for students who have been traditionally underserved or overlooked. Talent spotting is an intervention aimed at remedying underrepresentation. Myriad identification procedures are aimed at identifying students' cognitive abilities and achievement prior to providing exposure for all. Similar to other domains, talent spotting in education is a systematic procedure by which all students have access to intervention prior to gifted identification. Talent spotting permits students to grapple with the content while receiving supported instruction, all prior to gifted identification.

Implications for Other Districts

Districts may consider implementing talent development as a way to remedy underrepresentation. A primary step in talent development exploration includes reviewing the definition of giftedness at the local level to match the strengths and needs of the students in the district. Designing a definition for gifted and a philosophy for a program should include pathways and differentiated entry points for students with different readiness. Program administrators may start with a thorough analysis of their data to find discrepancies. As educators look at the rate of participation in gifted programs by students from all subgroups, they uncover their overlooked gems. The goal is representation in gifted programming that reflects the demographics of the school or district. This does not mean that there has to be an exact match in order to reach responsive participation. Following an analysis of the data, decisions must be made about the type of talent development program that will be the most effective intervention to bridge the gaps in gifted identification. Talent development programs with an emphasis on critical thinking can be a way to provide students with skills that are transferrable to content areas. When the threshold is adjusted to bypass the need for content mastery, students can have appropriate entry to rigorous learning experiences without the added weight of struggling through content. Educators must understand that even with enrichment for all, students may still need scaffolds to access the curriculum.

As educators configure their talent development programming, they will need to embed support aimed at students' social-emotional learning. Enrichment can be a way to tap student efficacy, allowing students to see how their thinking is the foundation for all learning. By intentionally emphasizing development of students' scholarly identities, educators will be able to meet students' psychosocial needs. Honoring the different manifestations of talent and the different times that said talents emerge is part of the desired outcome of talent development programs. Professional learning for educators is an area that needs to be differentiated to provide support for educators. A comprehensive rollout for talent development includes opportunities for educators to address any incorrect assumptions they have about CLED students. It is imperative that the implementation follow the vision and mission of the gifted department. Although students receiving services in talent development are not labelled gifted, students must be viewed as at-potential instead of at-risk. Educators will need to be able to embrace the unique platform of talent scouting.

Program administrators will need to know what sources of funding will be used to fund the program. With the revision and reauthorization of the Elementary and Secondary Education Act of 1965 (ESEA), the Every Student Succeeds Act (ESSA, 2015) includes provisions that support gifted and talented students. For the first time, ESSA specifically notes that districts may use Title I funds to identify and serve gifted and talented students. Talent development must be designed and implemented in such a way that it is seen as part of the continuum of advanced academics or gifted services.

This approach is preferred in that it honors the sentiment that educators realize giftedness occurs in all populations. Students are given the opportunity to build on skills that they already possess, abasing the deficit model that may erroneously be associated with students from diverse populations. Proponents of talent development realize the dexterity of talent development as it has been used in other disciplines outside of education with success. Additionally, this strategy aligns with the problem-solving model in schools. Students are provided consistent intervention with fidelity and go through progress monitoring. Ultimately, placement decisions are made based on the data explored through talent development intervention.

Other Important Considerations

Educators with specialized training—particularly in the delivery of enrichment skills that include but are not limited to divergent, convergent, evaluative, and visual thinking—provide ways for students to demonstrate what they are already able to do with thinking skills. Structure for talent development programs can vary extensively. To provide the greatest impact aimed at underrepresentation, a universal implementation ensures that all students at a grade level or levels have access to the instruction. This opportunity to be exposed to higher order thinking skills in a supportive yet demanding environment allows students to show skills and strengths that may not be tapped in the general education setting.

> *As students see themselves as capable, their willingness to engage in academic pursuits increases.*

Talent development instructional approaches that are not laden in core content areas appeal to students who may not see themselves as adept in school environments. Students are permitted to experience the intervention regardless of what their demonstrated achievement suggests. The goal is not to assess their achievement, but rather to cultivate potential. When skills such as critical thinking and problem solving are emphasized, students have an opportunity to demonstrate the strengths and the wide array of abilities they actually possess. These robust opportunities not only allow teachers to see students in a different light, but also allow students to see themselves as scholarly. As students see themselves as capable, their willingness to engage in academic pursuits increases. When social-emotional skills are also addressed within a talent development opportunity, students learn how to deal with psychosocial barriers that may impact the way they engage in academic settings.

Talent development involving thinking skills, engineering, or other real-world applications is enticing for students. Talent development experiences should be structured for learners to reach their full potential. Such advanced academic programs and resources enhance students' schooling. Students should be permitted to engage in academic pursuits that extend beyond the core experiences. Comprehensive approaches to talent development deliver personalized options and guidance in order to meet the needs of students. Talent development pathways lead students on a clearly articulated journey of intellectual, social, and emotional growth. Talent does not develop in isolation. Schools can and must support diverse learners by providing programming that allows students to discover their unique voice, explore opportunities, cultivate a love of learning, and become bold creative achievers and contributors.

| Talent does not develop in isolation.

In talent spotting, the goal is to provide exposure. Through academic behavioral observations, teachers are able to gain insight into a student's more comprehensive set of skills and abilities. Through direct instruction in specified skills—particularly ones that may serve as a potential pathway into gifted programming—students engage in content and delivery that are matched to their abilities. In order to give appropriate consideration for placement into gifted programs, all students (especially students who come from underrepresented backgrounds) benefit from having deliberate, well-thought-out talent development programming prior to gifted identification. Talent spotting is an effective intervention aimed at recognizing the hidden talents and students from underserved populations.

Talent development as a framework for gifted education honors that ability is malleable (Olszewski-Kubilius, Subotnik, & Worrell, 2018; Subotnik, Olszewski-Kubilius, & Worrell, 2011). By providing talent development as a framework, educators can honor the unique needs of gifted learners. Giftedness is widely recognized to manifest in multiple ways. Students can maximize their trajectory when provided opportunities that dismantle barriers. Talent development is an optimal way for educators to remedy for previous learning opportunities while guiding children's ability and cultivating their potential. Educators can not only focus on achievement, but also devote attention to psychosocial variables as determining factors in successful talent development. Because giftedness is developmental, the interaction of abilities and robust learning experiences is necessary for students to attain at levels that match their ability.

In the gifted education field, educators agree that intelligence is emergent and that it is fluid. Student intellect develops over time, it can be nurtured, and it manifests itself in different ways in different cultures. Culture may influence how intelligence is expressed. All of this leads to evidence that shows that intelligence is complex, and when looking at ability across diverse cultures, educators must use strategies that will provide platforms for students to demonstrate that intelligence is emergent. Access through challenging opportunities is beneficial to students. Opportunities through talent development enhance students' achievement, but talent development is not a pathway to gifted programming for everyone. Because giftedness is developmental, it is critical that talent development as systemic programming must be presented as early intervention. With extensive exposure, students are more likely to demonstrate achievement that matches their ability. Providing a platform rich in creativity recognizes the importance of the creative process. Such an embrace positions educators to support direct instruction that supports students to use creative thinking and problem solving to reach deeper levels of understanding.

REFLECTION QUESTIONS

1. Why is it critical to expose younger students to various talent domains?

2. Given that giftedness is developmental, how does that impact the need for talent development as an option for gifted learners, particularly with regard to equity in gifted education?

3. What experiences have you had with students from diverse backgrounds that reinforce the importance of understanding that previous learning can be a barrier to attainment?

CHAPTER 5

Race

To avoid conflating race and class, please note that although overlap exists in some instances, educators cannot assume causation. When compared to their more economically advantaged peers, students from economically vulnerable backgrounds are significantly less likely to be identified for gifted programming. Each year that schools fail to serve high-potential students who are economically vulnerable is a loss. Children from poverty represent a significant number of students who make up the pipeline of untapped potential. Considering that about one-quarter of public schools are high poverty (McFarland et al., 2019), poverty must be addressed as educators pursue equitable participation in gifted programs.

The Effects of Racialized Outcomes

Racialized outcomes consistently and disproportionately impact academic attainment for culturally, linguistically, and economically diverse students. As noted previously, in the 2013–2014 school year, Black (15.5%) and Latino (24.8%) students made up 40.3% of the public school population, but they only made up 28% of students in gifted programs (U.S. Department of Education, Office for Civil Rights, 2014). This mismatch is grossly unjust. Giftedness occurs in all demographics, so the degree to which educators recognize and identify giftedness in students from diverse backgrounds is a source of concern.

Several known factors contribute to this disproportionately low rate. With highly segregated public school systems, Black and Latino children are less likely to participate in gifted programs even if they attend a school with such programs. Studies (Gershenson et al., 2016) also show that Black children have a higher chance of being identified for gifted programs if they have at least one Black teacher. Consider the demographics of the teaching force in the U.S.: During the 2011–2012 school year, 82% of public school teachers were White, while 51% percent of elementary and secondary students were White. Black teachers made up 7% of the workforce and Hispanic teachers made up 8%, while Black students made up 16% of the student population and Hispanic students made up 24%. By 2024, White students are estimated to represent 46% of the student population (U.S. Department of Education, 2016). The disparities mean that Black children can matriculate through U.S. public schools without ever having a teacher of color. The impact of that plausible scenario has significant influence on the educational attainment for Black children.

Black students are overrepresented in special education, while underrepresented in gifted programs.

Focusing on gifted education, the lens for examining educators' collective work is curtailed by a lack of cultural proficiency. The policies and practices developed in gifted education have an adverse impact on students, and they reinforce notions of otherness and invisibility. Interestingly enough, similar disproportionality occurs in student discipline and other areas. Black students are overrepresented in special education, while underrepresented in gifted programs. Some children of color are potentially being misunderstood. Their perceived negative traits happening in their school experience could actually speak to giftedness.

Overcoming Bias and Addressing Equity

Navigating the American educational system is challenging at best. Educational outcomes and experiences are significantly impacted by variables that are out of students' realm of control. Values are an inherent part of culture, and school culture is informed by a culture of privilege, Whiteness, and middle-class values. The delusional approach of a post-racial society fuels the wheels of injustice perpetuated in the nation's schools. Although schools are a system, systems are run by people. Therefore, educators have the responsibility of dismantling biased systems that disproportionately affect children of color. The myth of colorblindness asserts that individuals do not see color or race; instead, they see that people are all the same. This is fraught with fallacy. Racialized outcomes in education have been duly noted, and they continue to persist in spite of growing evidence of ways to combat such wrongs. Racial characteristics are visible and should not be ignored. As a Black educator, I feel that for others to say that they do not see color when they see me is to suggest that they fail to acknowledge the totality of my identity, thus erasing my existence. People are not all the same, and to attempt to espouse such rhetoric further besets the work of equity and access in education.

The starting line of the race is different for students from diverse backgrounds. In many instances, CLED students negotiate a superfluous dance. Carrying the extra weight they shoulder as students from marginalized groups, they may feel the need or have an expectation placed on them to conform to a way of doing school that does not honor their cultural identity, leading to learning that is emotionally taxing. These students may lack a sense of agency that is necessary for them to bring all of who they are into the learning environment. Such agency is necessary to contribute to class and be fully present in the environment. This barrier of having to learn while navigating barriers and dealing with stereotypes is manifest in the dominant society's view of how those issues affect marginalized students.

Acceptance based on students' behavior or conduct is rooted in respectability politics. I have observed this and have even participated in it to some degree. The challenge with this notion is that it further oppresses students from marginalized groups, asserting fallacies about their worth and how they measure up to their counterparts. Additionally, respectability politics relieve people from dominant culture of the responsibility to dismantle systems of oppression (O'Neal, 2018). Feelings of marginality may arise when students know multiple cultures but do not experience being entirely accepted by members of either culture, essentially because they could function in the other culture. Many of our students from diverse populations mesh the distinct worlds in which they operate so they experience dualism. This prohibits them from gaining an authentic sense of self. An approach that guides students and educators through these experiences is one that focuses on a commitment to become culturally proficient.

People are not all the same, and to attempt to espouse such rhetoric further besets the work of equity and access in education.

The goal of this work is to probe educators' collective conscience to realize barriers that preclude access to vital learning environments for a significant portion of America's students. Although the content causes discomfort, the endeavor is not to suggest blame or induce guilt. The desired outcome is that educators all leave gifted education better than they found it. That may mean revisiting thoughts and beliefs that are not equitable. This does not suggest that the field is racist, but it does highlight the egregious errors that have been carried on the backs of students from marginalized groups. Overwhelmingly, Black and Latino students are denied access to learning environments that are matched to their readiness, resulting in untapped potential. The result is a concentration of untapped potential that could be utilized to improve all aspects of the human condition.

The human brain is wired to recognize differences. The degree to which educators allow those differences to inform attitudes and beliefs about how they interact with students, and further limit or constrain their experiences, introduces the element of biases. Everyone has biases. The extent to which you, as an educator, check those biases is where the forceful power in humanity takes preeminence. To fully acknowledge the current narrative, one that is overwhelmingly unjust to students of color, "it is important to note that not all gifted children look or act alike. Giftedness exists in every demographic group and personality type" (NAGC, n.d.-b, para. 3). As varied as cultures are, to define giftedness on the basis of the predominance of traits from the dominant, some might say oppressive, culture is inherently a racist practice. Giftedness mirrors the experiences of the extensive cultures that comprise the collective student body in America's classrooms. There is an indelible divide drawn by the color line. Persistent gaps (belief, opportunity, achievement, and excellence) exist between White and non-Asian minority students. Equal opportunity in education does not broadly exist. Factors attributed to the unequal outcomes of children of color in America's schools include implicit and explicit bias, and teacher quality.

Microaggressions are another layer of harm that diverse students may be subjected to. Microaggressions are specific remarks, questions, or actions that can happen casually, frequently, and often without any harm intended in everyday life. Microaggressions are painful because they have to do with a person's membership in a group that is discriminated against or subjected to stereotypes. In search of educational equity, learning environments are needed in which:

> educational policies, practices, interactions, and
> resources, are representative of, constructed by, and

responsive to all people such that each individual
has access to, can participate, and make progress
in high-quality learning experiences that empower
them towards self-determination and reduces
disparities in outcomes regardless of individual
characteristics and cultural identities. (Skelton &
Warren, 2016, p. 9)

The Gifted Equity Model

A framework for practical steps to address underrepresentation,
the Gifted Equity Model (GEM; see Figure 1) provides an overview
to understand underrepresentation, as well as guided steps to enact
change resulting in improved educational outcomes for students
who have been traditionally left out of gifted programs. This model
was adapted from Coleman's (2019) research on diversifying science, technology, engineering, and mathematics (STEM) education,
which highlights the development of a plan to increase diversity in
STEM through equitable practices. In evaluating progress toward
adequate representation, the goal is to access untapped potential in
gifted learners, especially those from historically underserved populations. By elevating the infrastructure of procedures, practices,
and infrastructure aimed at honoring diverse gifted learners, a clear
intervention with timeless impact emerges. This notion of opening
doors is characterized by achieving racial equity in gifted education and a racially responsive collaborative approach to gifted services with the eventual outcome of increasing student belonging for
those who have previously been locked out of gifted programming.

Barriers are invisible except to the individuals whose efforts
are curtailed by their presence. When educators accept that school
systems are designed to serve students with mainstream identities,
they develop an understanding of why certain gaps exist. Some
of the barriers have become particularly evident. Students from
diverse cultures demonstrate behaviors that may be rooted in cultural foundations. Educators' lack of cultural awareness can con-

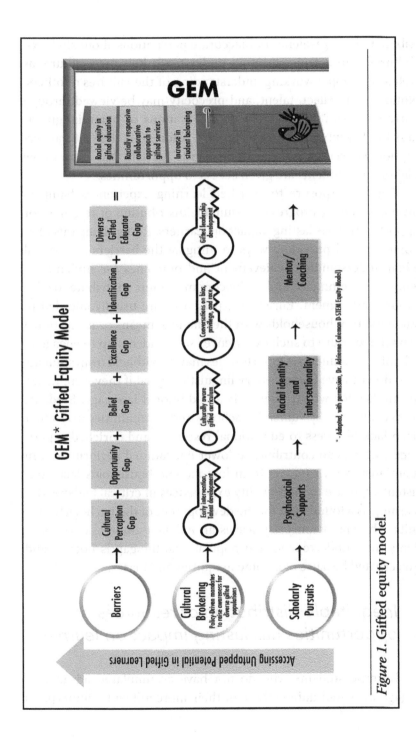

Figure 1. Gifted equity model.

tribute to the prevalence of inaccurate perceptions about students. Culturally proficient educators understand their own culture, as well as develop a working understanding of the cultures of others. Notions of intellect, talent, and precocity may be viewed through narrow lenses that constrain demonstrations of potential giftedness by students from diverse groups. Addressing the cultural perception gap serves as a way to dismantle barriers that impact how high-ability students are given access to opportunities.

Lack of exposure to enriched learning experiences hampers diverse students' progress. Inequitable distribution of resources or opportunities has lasting impact on learners. Recognizing this phenomenon and providing ways to mitigate the barriers are critical when understanding achievement and outcomes for students for whom race, ethnicity, and socioeconomic status contribute to educational attainment. Enriched experiences are usually afforded to students from households with the financial means or navigational capital. Exposure to such experiences sets students up to engage in school environments. Opportunities may be withheld from students who do not have the necessary linguistic capital if they were raised in families for whom English is an additional language. Students from economically vulnerable schools and communities may suffer from lack of access to educational resources and enriched experiences, which can contribute to lower educational performance. In many instances, students from low-income households lack consistent exposure to high-quality experiences in critical and creative learning as a foundation for the development of their scholarly pursuits. The opportunity gap leaves an indelible impression on students from underrepresented populations; the gap is notable and exacerbated because of income inequities and biases.

Inequitable distribution of resources or opportunities has lasting impact on learners.

Because students who do not have accumulated advantages engage in school differently than their more affluent counterparts who have benefits and privilege, educators may have different levels of expectations and beliefs about the students' capabilities. Often, such students are capable of performing and achieving at higher levels than others perceive. This belief gap results in mismatching and undermatching. Students end up enrolled in courses that do not match their potential and preclude them from maximizing their potential.

When students are not exposed to the proper educational environment, they are not exposed to enriched content. The heavy emphasis on minimum competency has far-reaching impacts on achievement. The disparity in the percentage of students from economically vulnerable environments compared to higher income students who reach advanced levels of academic performance is egregious. Under ESSA (2015), states are focusing attention on high-ability learners from all demographics; new requirements around tracking and reporting are causing states to pay attention to what is happening to diverse learners in an effort to close the excellence gap. In large part, gifted identification uses information related to achievement and standards set forth from national normative data. Given the scope of inequities associated with income and achievement, students from diverse backgrounds are left out of the identification pool. The identification gap is the result of the aforementioned gaps, resulting in culturally and linguistically diverse students from economically vulnerable backgrounds being absent from gifted identification. But they are hidden in plain sight.

With effective cultural brokering and enhanced policy-driven mandates, educators can raise awareness of diverse gifted populations. With consistent and early interventions, students can be provided requisite opportunities for their talents to develop and be nurtured. The pathway from talent development to gifted services permits educators to meet the needs of gifted learners from all backgrounds. Diverse gifted learners thrive in educational environments in which culturally aware gifted curriculum is implemented with fidelity. As educators have conversations about bias, privilege, and race, they sharpen their skills and subsequently position themselves to more adeptly meet the needs of CLED students. Inputs in cultural brokering result in educators being apprised of meeting the needs of diverse gifted learners.

As students are provided supports in scholarly pursuits, they develop strategies that enable them to fully participate in gifted programming. The attention to the affective domain—including guidance in self-concept, self-esteem, and how to navigate social institutions—provides the scaffolding necessary for students to reach their fullest potential. When students are provided with support for them to understand racial identity and intersectionality, they gain the skills to address social injustices, solve social problems, and tap their potential. With effective mentoring and coaching, students traverse through gifted environments in ways that honor and reinforce their exceptional ability.

Educators need to dissect the ways in which race, ethnicity, socioeconomic status, English proficiency, social capital, cultural capital, or other factors affect equity and opportunity gaps. Addressing gaps is necessary to identify untapped potential in gifted learners without viewing them through a deficit lens. Combined, trends that arise from these gaps suggest that some educators do not understand how much students from impoverished environments can achieve. *Impoverished* may describe students' environments, but it does not adequately describe students.

Consider the intricacies of teaching and learning, and juxtapose those with layers of complexity that come in the form of differences by race, ethnicity, and linguicism. The National Center for Education Statistics (de Brey et al., 2019) estimated that in fall 2018, about 56.6 million students attended elementary and secondary schools. Extend the reach by considering the reported racial demographics of that cohort: The percentage of Black students enrolled in public schools was 15%, White students 49%, Hispanic 26%, American Indian/Alaskan Native around 1%, Asian/Pacific Islander 5%, and students who are of two or more races 3%. Racial identity and cultural awareness pose a significant learning curve for the proponents of equity in gifted education.

REFLECTION QUESTIONS

1. What are the top three identifiers you would use to describe yourself?

2. When was the first time you were made aware of your race?

3. Who are the underserved in your school?

4. What supports or targeted interventions are in place in your school aimed at providing access to gifted services for students from underserved populations?

CHAPTER 6

Understanding Privilege and Implicit Bias

Privilege imposes a weight on those who do not benefit from privilege. This weight carried on the backs of diverse students severely constrains their access to gifted programming. Part of the solution to underrepresentation includes developing awareness of privilege and understanding the hidden consequences of asserted values and beliefs so that they are no longer the foundation for practices and policies in gifted education. Raising awareness about privilege is not intended to assign guilt or shame. The goal is to reduce the adverse impact of privilege on those who do not have the same level of social capital as those benefitting from privilege. Some students do not have access to requisite experiences and resources due to obstacles that are placed in their way.

Recognizing Privilege

Privilege is a right or immunity granted as a particular benefit, advantage, or favor that one does not earn. It can be considered a right or benefit that is given to some people and not to others. In education—particularly within gifted education—the advantage that wealthy and empowered people have over other people in the same environment who do not have the same social or economic capital is notable. As a community, educators can see privilege alive and thriving in gifted education. As adept as educators are at recognizing privilege, they must begin to ask questions that dismantle the system in order to enact change that will move the pendulum in gifted education. Privilege can be used as a force to disrupt the status quo. As you read this chapter, keep the following questions in mind.

1. What does it mean to be privileged?
2. What does it mean to be marginalized? Who is usually marginalized?
3. What are the ways people tend to deny that privilege is occurring?
4. What happens when one group is privileged over another?
5. What action can you take to interrupt the cycles of oppression and inequality?

Increasing the public urgency to meet the needs of gifted children must include an awareness of privilege and the impact of that privilege on underrepresented populations.

Implications of Race and Recognizing Exceptionality

As noted previously, Black students are 54% less likely than their White peers to be identified for gifted education (Nicholson-Crotty et al., 2016). This has colossal implications for educational attainment—a ticket to a different kind of education. Research also finds that Black students are 3 times more likely to be placed in a gifted program if they have a teacher who is also African American. Considering the demographics of teachers in the United States juxtaposed with the demographics of students in the United States, the likelihood of Black and brown children having a teacher who looks like them is slim.

Responsive pedagogy in gifted education is instrumental at remedying underrepresentation. This requires that educators shift their thinking as they look at the goals and expectations of gifted programs as they reflect the needs of diverse communities. From there, educators have to look at themselves because they are a part of the problem, and acknowledging that is part of the solution. Educators can begin by having courageous conversations about their students, which means that they need to have courageous conversations about race, culture, and difference. Through these conversations, they will learn a significant amount about their students. Educators also need to learn about what they know and do not know about students' cultural diversity. The fundamental disconnect in gifted education is that programs are aimed at identifying and serving students with mainstream identities. This is a concept that strains students' abilities to fully engage in an academic environment. When educators accept that school systems are designed to serve students with mainstream identities—meaning White, middle and upper class, and English speaking—they will understand why the opportunity gap exists. Schools and systems must examine the ways in which they can change how they operate in order to meet the needs of the most marginalized students. I believe that, until students with the most marginalized backgrounds are served in gifted education, educators have not reached equitable practices.

Given the diversity of experiences, backgrounds, and opportunities, educators must adopt policies and practices that recognize and value the diversity that their students bring to the classroom.

There is a racialized construct of exceptionality. Many educators view exceptionality through the lens of White, middle-class experiences. Yet, educators recognize that ability is contextual. Given the diversity of experiences, backgrounds, and opportunities, educators must adopt policies and practices that recognize and value the diversity that their students bring to the classroom. A critical shift in the work toward equity in gifted education is maintaining a systems focus. This focus allows district- and school-level educators to share the acknowledgment that there is something wrong with the educational system as it pertains to gifted education. This shift involves moving away from a deficit model that focuses on the weaknesses of students from diverse backgrounds. In order to address problems and systems, there must be a systemic solution. This means that educators can no longer blame students, families, and communities for racial disparities or any other disparities in student achievement and access to gifted education.

Instead, educators must focus on the structural barriers that prevent students of color and students from marginalized identities from achieving academic success at the same levels as White students and students with other mainstream identities. Until educators fully advocate for serving students from diverse backgrounds in gifted education, equity in gifted programs will not be achieved. Issues of inequality and equity pedagogy are complex, and educators must not settle for easy answers to difficult questions. This requires the elimination of inequities that contribute to disproportionate access to gifted programming and, ultimately, achievement by certain students. The time to act is now.

Addressing School Climate

Education continues to be one of the greatest civil rights fights. This means that educators and other stakeholders must have frank, hard dialogue about the climate for underserved students with the goal of effecting a change in thinking, language, and actions. Educators must invest in culturally aware practices that lead to the success of underserved students and, ultimately, of all students. Educators can accomplish this by setting and monitoring equity-minded goals, as well as allocating aligned resources to achieve them. Individuals with the responsibility of facilitating and administering gifted programs must develop and actively pursue a clear vision and goals for achieving high-quality experiences. A vigilant monitoring of data is needed to ensure equitable participation and achievement among underserved students in gifted programs. School climate is a window to racial equity.

Educators must invest in culturally aware practices that lead to the success of underserved students and, ultimately, of all students.

When properly collected, this disaggregated and analyzed assessment of school climate may give additional insight into equity in gifted education. Educators must shift the way they assess climate to intentionally focus on the experience of students with marginalized identities in gifted education. This type of change can only happen when there is a commitment to equity from the top of an organization. Leadership is critical in the development of core beliefs around gifted education. Part of the core beliefs must include understanding that high-ability learners require differentiated curriculum and extended opportunities. Educators must demonstrate their belief that all students should be able to engage in gifted education and experiences that emphasize the development of higher level thinking processes across content, intellectual innovation, research, and communication skills that utilize technology and creativity. Because schools are based on majority identity, their decision making is fundamentally flawed. They are fundamentally designed to duplicate how they have been making decisions all along.

As the paradigm on how educators view students from diverse backgrounds shifts, educators invite the opportunity to implement strategies focused on providing access that is warranted for underrepresented learners. Due to the nature of social justice education, discomfort should be expected. Working through the discomfort, not avoiding or settling, sanctions opportunities to disrupt the status quo of gifted education. Some individuals in dominant culture find it difficult when confronted with the imbalance and reallocation of resources they have grown accustomed to. Establishing trust and rapport is vital to the success of social justice work in gifted education.

Recognizing how bias runs interference in gifted education is a central point of understanding. Oftentimes, when a cultural conflict ensues in a classroom, educators are disconnected and do not have a robust understanding of the backgrounds of the students they serve. The intersectionality of identities is critical to understanding multicultural education. Part of cultural brokering involves educators recognizing their limitations and identifying and serving students from backgrounds that are different from theirs. Advocacy is critical to remedying underrepresentation.

In order to find overlooked gems sitting in the seats of your classrooms today, there are fruitful areas you must be aware of in your systems data set. By taking a look at your disproportionality in student discipline, flags may be raised that will prompt you to consider the disconnect for students who are overrepresented in student discipline but underrepresented in gifted programming. Taking into consideration data revealed through student observation checklists, one must recognize the limits. Individuals completing the observation checklists are only privy to their own worldview—that worldview may be one that has had limited exposure to students from diverse backgrounds, one that maybe laden with biases, and one that looks at students from diverse backgrounds through a deficit model. That furthers the underrepresentation of students from diverse backgrounds.

Advocacy is critical to remedying underrepresentation.

The impact of culture is widely represented in all aspects of students' identity at school. Part of the work in uncovering blind spots is raising the level of awareness in your school district or system of the areas and programming that adversely impact access for students and underrepresented populations. Blind spots grow from situations you just do not know about that have a consistent and persistent impact on specific populations. As you consider leveraging equity and access for all learners in gifted programming, an analysis of your data is a critical undertaking. In order to make notable progress, you must suspend your disbelief and exchange judgment for curiosity, or wonderment. Embarking upon wonderment facilitates the movement for you and other stakeholders to get to those deeper places of understanding and address the blind spots in gifted education. Yes, gifted education has made progress as a field, but there is an inordinate amount of work that has yet to be done. Part of remedying underrepresentation in gifted education includes exploration of cultures, checking biases, examining privilege, and building relationships.

REFLECTION QUESTIONS

1. What does it mean to be privileged?

2. Who tends to be marginalized? What does it mean to be marginalized?

3. What are the ways you or other educators tend to deny that privilege is occurring?

4. What happens when one group is privileged over another?

5. How can you take action to interrupt the cycles of oppression and inequality in gifted education?

CHAPTER 7

Empowering Educators to Make a Difference

Moving forward with the work of accessing the pipelines of untapped potential, early intervention is a critical step in the process. With the use of responsive interventions that include enrichment for all learners, educators will position the most vulnerable learners to display the amazing talents they possess. Through the effective allocation of resources to some of the schools with the greatest needs and as educators equitably distribute funds to areas that give students exposure to creative and critical thinking in direct instruction, educators will see a return on the investment.

Building Culturally Responsive Pedagogy

By having equitable access to high-quality and culturally aware instruction, curriculum, and other educational resources, gifted educators can create pathways to success while addressing student needs through innovative programming and resources. District and school leaders must provide professional learning to strengthen teachers' knowledge and skills in eliminating disparities in achievement based on race and/or ethnicity. This work will be instrumental in remedying any practices that lead to overrepresentation of students of color in special education and discipline. Additionally, it will be gamechanging in that it will support the remediation of practices that lead to underrepresentation of students of color in programs such as gifted, honors academies, and Advanced Placement courses.

Teachers should also be instructed in best practices for identifying students for gifted programming. Although tests and assessments are tools for identifying gifted students, they should not be the sole source of identification. The use of multiple measures for identifying students is a strategy that allows multiple data points to be considered and necessitates cultural competence on the behalf of the individuals who teach students and subsequently nominate or refer students for gifted programs.

Through culturally responsive pedagogy, students from diverse backgrounds have an opportunity to enter learning environments in which their strengths are seen as skills related to the academic environment. They will be seen as capable and able to achieve at high levels with the commensurate level of support that matches teacher expectations. Educators need to draw from students' funds of knowledge and construct learning experiences that are connected to students' lived experiences and honor their cultural capital. By doing so, educators will recognize the strengths students bring from their lived experiences and will be able to connect with those experiences in meaningful ways throughout the learning environment.

Tapping students' funds of knowledge is part of a strengths-based approach to teaching, as educators endeavor to connect learning experiences to what students already know. Students do not show up to school as empty vessels for educators to fill, but rather as producers of knowledge waiting for educators to connect the learning in meaningful ways. This is helpful in that it promotes meaningful participation from all students, and multiple perspectives are valued and proposed. Students must see themselves in all aspects of the curricular materials and standards. All curriculum and instruction materials and standards addressed must reflect the unique cultural and linguistic diversity of the student population.

All learners must be held to higher expectations.

Culturally responsive pedagogy uses diverse learners' cultural knowledge, prior experiences, and performance styles to make learning more appropriate and effective. It requires educators to teach to the strengths of students and through the strengths of students. The opposite, and what is seen all too often in classrooms, is the deficit model, which further divides and abases groups by focusing on what students do not yet know or have not yet demonstrated. All learners must be held to higher expectations. The expectations must be reflective of students' readiness and diversity, and the understanding of how members from various cultures or groups do school. The key to maximizing this balance is through support and high expectations. In looking at students who are learning English as an additional language, specific understanding must be clarified around the nature of second-language acquisition. Value must be given to the native language foundation. Bridging and making effective transition across the languages is essential.

In addition to nurturing academic skills, educators must also address gifted students' noncognitive or psychosocial skills. Diverse students' racial and psychological development is as necessary to attend to as other topics in underrepresentation. Focusing on social-emotional skills, such as self-concept, self-esteem, and other variables, is necessary when considering how children of color experience gifted education. Students need to be in learning environments in which they are free to learn without the weight of stereotype threat (i.e., the belief that their performance will be attributed to their whole group). Black students may struggle with a sense of belonging and have difficulty balancing peer relations and their overall group affiliation. Black students who do well in school may experience an ambivalence and affective dissonance with regard to academic effort and success. Additionally, Black students may face challenges balancing their participation in multiple worlds and how they choose to perform in order to maintain positive relations in peer groups. This can cause dissonance, and students may require support and strategies to learn how to effectively cope with multiple worlds and balancing their identity throughout their diverse experiences. Exceptionality can be misconstrued for "acting White," and students may risk being alienated and experiencing negative peer relations. The more that students of color see themselves in the curricular experiences in their gifted environment, with the contributions of their race acknowledged, the more they experience a greater sense of belonging in gifted programs.

Raising Awareness of Privilege

The weight of privilege and bias on the identity of diverse learners has far-reaching consequences. Raising awareness of privilege affords educators opportunities to uncover hidden biases that lead to values and beliefs that may make up systemic practices and policies in gifted education. Part of redesigning programming to promote more equitable access includes reducing implicit bias in gifted education. Behaviors must be viewed through a culturally aware lens. When students and teachers are from different backgrounds, the opportunity for cultural conflict to ensue is notably high.

Gifted education is only as equitable as the students with the most marginalized identities experience it to be. Education continues to be a great equalizer. The achievement gap spells out the discrepancy of performance for minority learners who demonstrate academic prowess at higher levels of proficiency. Gifted educators must mind the "other" gap. Understanding the excellence gap shines additional light on the impact of poverty, as well as students' previous learning experiences. Because gifted students are in all populations, participation in gifted programming should reflect the population of a school or a district. When this reflection is not adequate, there is underrepresentation. Overwhelmingly, students who are Black, Latino, or from free and reduced meals programs are left out or locked out of programming. Because the American educational system is achieving exactly what it was designed to do, gifted educators must disrupt the system in the spirit of advocacy.

> *Part of addressing biases is seeking out interaction with people different from you—people who are of different races, cultures, or linguistic backgrounds.*

Part of the work in disrupting or dismantling this system is recognizing the impact of microaggressions on students from underserved backgrounds. Microaggressions are the kinds of remarks, questions, or actions that are painful because they have to do with a person's membership in a group that is discriminated against or subjected to stereotypes, frequently and often without any harm intended, in everyday life. In brokering systems that are more equitable and providing students with more comfortable and accessible learning environments, educators must be constantly vigilant of their own biases. These are attitudes, stereotypes, and assumptions educators are not even aware of that can creep into their minds and ultimately affect their actions. Part of addressing biases is seeking out interaction with people different from you—people who are of different races, cultures, or linguistic backgrounds. Individuals from more privileged backgrounds must understand their positions of power and not be defensive about their privilege.

Be open to discussing your own attitudes and biases and how they might have hurt others or, in some sense, revealed bias on your part. I encourage you to be an ally in attaining equity in gifted education by standing against all forms of bias and racism. Because privilege is invisible to some, you must recognize the barriers to gifted programming—the barriers that are invisible unless you encounter them personally. Addressing the myth of colorblindness is part of the work that is central to providing equitable access in gifted education. Colorblindness is counterproductive and actually contributes to racism. Colorblindness invalidates peoples' identities. Denying people their identities is not racial progress. This also promotes racial avoidance. Race is also intimately tied to identities and signifies culture, tradition, language, and heritage, which are genuine sources of pride. Like many other factors, such as gender, religion, or socioeconomic status, race is a basic element that makes up your being, whether or not you consciously acknowledge its role in your life. Colorblindness is appreciated because it purports to take race off the table, but in actuality, it is an attempt to erase a significant portion of one's identity. Colorblind ideology is fraught with problems and pitfalls. Cultural awareness is a more progressive approach to evaluating the diversity and inclusion for individuals from different backgrounds.

Next Steps

Identify a way for your district to move your procedures into policy in order to substantiate the level of programming with a focus around equity in and access to gifted education. Look for areas in which your program may be strengthened by increasing policies aimed at diversity. Engage in ongoing review of your practices and be aware of where discrepancies are happening. Challenge implementations that are rooted in bias or produce inequities. Develop allies who will be willing to operationalize messaging consistent with equity and access in gifted education. Expose blind spots in favor of embedding necessary supports that permit students from marginalized groups to access gifted services. Consider using different funding sources to identify and serve gifted learners. For example, see how your school's Title I funds can be used for supplemental services for gifted learners. You can also follow the ABCs of achieving equity outlined in Figure 2.

Meeting the needs of gifted learners does not stop at the end of the school day. Supplemental programs on weekends and during the summer are ways to allow students to fully engage in developing and nurturing their giftedness. Implement differentiated outreach efforts to establish connections with families and community part-

The ABCs of Achieving Equity

A. Access is granted through meaningful and purposeful strategies. Educators have the power to recognize barriers that may preclude underrepresented students from fully participating in gifted programs.

B. Recognize **biases**. Check your own biases in an effort to espouse multicultural equity. Address **blind spots**; suspend your disbelief in exchange for curiosity. Although **barriers** exist, they can be dismantled.

C. As an early intervention, develop a **critical mass** of students by frontloading experiences in critical and creative thinking as a potential pathway to gifted programming for students from diverse populations. **Colorblindness** is a myth. It invalidates people's identities, purports to take race off the table, and is fraught with problems and pitfalls. Educators can act as **cultural brokers** for individuals who are from marginalized groups.

D. Discover the hidden talents in diverse gifted learners. Provide platforms for these learners to engage in program models that offer a pedagogy of plenty. **Deliver** a continuum of gifted services aimed at meeting students' needs rather than forcing students to fit inside rigid programs. **Determine** identification protocol using local normative data.

E. Achieve **equity** in gifted programs by addressing values, beliefs, practices, and policies that exclude students from certain groups from participating in gifted programs. **Exposure** is critical in achieving equity. Provide students with experiences that allow them to develop their potential.

F. Frontloading, or talent development, is a way to increase the number of underrepresented students in advanced academic programs through direct instruction.

Figure 2. The ABCs of achieving equity.

G. Giftedness is developmental and occurs in all populations. Giftedness may manifest differently across language, socioeconomic status, and race and ethnicity. Culturally proficient educators understand the impact of culture on how students "do school."

H. Highlight awareness of the unique needs of gifted learners with attention devoted to the understanding of the needs of gifted learners from diverse populations. **Hold** all learners to high expectations with commensurate support.

I. Identities are complex, and students have multiple identities. The intersectionality of their identities requires culturally proficient educators to tap students' potential in order for them to achieve at levels that honor their academic trajectory.

J. See disproportionality in gifted education as a social **justice** agenda. Discover ways to embed equity access in all facets of gifted programming.

K. Keep equity at the forefront of your policies and practices.

L. The use of **local norms**, ranked performance at the building level, is a way to address disproportionality. By comparing students to peers with comparable experiences and backgrounds, equitable access to gifted education is provided.

M. Change **mindset** about equity in gifted education by seeing students from a strengths-based approach and recognizing the promise and ability they possess.

N. Support students as they develop and utilize **navigational capital** and get used to navigating social institutions, including educational spaces.

O. Opportunities are essential to cultivating talent. Students must be exposed to rich learning environments in order for them to develop and maximize their potential. **Overlooked**

Figure 2. Continued.

gems result when educators do not realize how cultural perceptions impact students' attainment.

P. Use **privilege** (a right or immunity granted as a particular benefit, advantage, or favor) to give others access to experiences that they are consistently and disproportionately denied.

Q. Quit seeing giftedness through a fixed mindset. Giftedness is developmental.

R. Responsive pedagogy requires educators to make a shift in their thinking. Expand access for gifted services by intervening early to permit scholars from diverse backgrounds to grow.

S. Shift from a deficit focus (i.e., "there is something wrong with these students") to a **systemic focus** (i.e., "there is something wrong with educational systems because they only serve students from dominant groups"). Through adaptive solutions, educators will learn a lot about students. Look at yourself and how you may be contributing to the inequities you see. Have courageous conversations about race, culture, and difference.

T. Talent development is a viable intervention that can be a gamechanger for increasing diversity in gifted education. This potential pathway promotes excellence for all learners and nurtures talent in students who perform or demonstrate the ability to perform beyond peers from comparable background and experiences.

U. Underrepresentation does not have to happen. Being cognizant of the causes of underrepresentation is helpful in improving intercultural skills. Use multicultural education as a support to increase the participation of diverse students in gifted education. Exploring issues of race and White privilege is not intended to assign guilt or shame, but rather to raise awareness.

Figure 2. Continued.

V. View gifted programming as a right for learners regardless of their racial, ethnic, linguistic, or socioeconomic status. See **value** in diversity in gifted education.

W. Write culturally aware gifted policies and have them codified in school board policy to ensure the perpetuity of gifted programming at the local level.

X. Remember that all learners must be held to higher **expectations**.

Y. Young scholars deserve to learn in educational environments that honor their talents and abilities.

Z. With the right combination of strategy, advocacy, and **zeal**, educators can do something about underrepresentation.

Figure 2. Continued.

ners as part of the support system for gifted students. Host parent meetings to provide them with a forum for networking; ensure diverse representation for the group. Form partnerships with centers for gifted education in your area to provide professional learning opportunities for educators and administrators through the use of Title II funds. Participate with networks of gifted educators at the state level, join your state affiliate organization for gifted children, and become active with understanding your state's legislative process as it pertains to meeting the needs of gifted learners. Through attending conferences, you may develop professional learning communities in which you will be able to sharpen your knowledge of gifted education.

Gifted education as a field is not racist, but there are many potential racialized outcomes. Students experience educational environments differently based on their experiences, and students perform differently on tests, interventions, and activities because educators may treat diverse learners differently than other students. Although these interactions may not be racist, they certainly can be an indication of bias that has gone unchecked. In District U-46, we have worked to uncover blind spots in our gifted programming. A blind spot is an area in which you may not know what you do not know, which means you will not be able to address an issue without careful investigation.

There are practical considerations for programming and implementation in order to deliver high-quality services for all learners. Limited previous opportunities for learning and diverse background experiences, coupled with a lack of cultural awareness from educators, are factors that decisively constrain the performance and demonstration of cognition for low-income or African American and Latino students. Economically vulnerable students or students with diverse learning experiences have accumulated disadvantage in the area of academic pursuits. Gifted educators can change the narrative when they see diverse learners through a funds of knowledge lens (i.e., seeing students as having potential giftedness that speaks to promise). When educators shift their focus from a deficit model of thinking to more of a strengths-based approach, they unveil opportunities and provide access, which are two critical levels of programming for underrepresented learners.

Achieving equity in gifted education requires a social justice agenda.

Poverty is insidious. Children from households that are economically vulnerable may have their talents masked or hidden by barriers. This opportunity gap exists prior to students attending school or as early as kindergarten. Consider the word gap evident in toddlers. Students from higher income families have higher vocabulary development compared to their peers from low-income households (Colker, 2014; Hart & Risley, 2003). Income disparity is prevalent in the U.S., which can be attributed to gaps in access to high-quality childcare. Students from households that are economically vulnerable are affected in a number of ways that impact their educational attainment. In order to equalize or level the playing field, supportive structures, such as talent development, must be implemented as a way to give access to students who have not had the same previous opportunities to learn. Gaps are evident early, and interventions aimed at closing the gaps must also be provided early.

Achieving equity in gifted education requires a social justice agenda. Reorganizing the way gifted programming is designed is the key to achieving different results. Promoting excellence helps to get the stakeholder buy-in that is necessary to address the gifted gap. Moving everybody up includes moving students from diverse populations into excellence groups. Lifting the equity agenda does not disadvantage anyone. If all students were born with life experiences that allowed them to have similar results, then barriers would not preclude certain groups' access to gifted education.

Educators can do things differently to equalize the playing field for diverse learners. Advocating for greater resources often matters, but even without many resources, change can occur. Understanding giftedness and valuing differences across cultures can open educators' eyes to the possibility and promise in overlooked gems. Talent development as a framework allows students' ability to grow in areas in which they exercise it. Structuring opportunities in which students are able to work hard and long to develop their skills with guided support and high expectations is a way to open doors for students from historically underserved populations. Creating opportunity and creating connections are ways that educators can inspire, focus, enable and express agency. A vision for gifted programming that accurately reflects students from all racial and ethnic backgrounds is plausible. The time to act is now; it is incumbent upon educators to implement systemic approaches to honor the talent from students from groups that have been consistently and disproportionately underserved in gifted education.

REFLECTION QUESTIONS

1. How do schools build trust with students from diverse backgrounds who have experienced systemic racism so that they may participate in gifted services?

2. What types of professional learning are effective for teachers and administrators who work with racially diverse students?

3. How do educators develop and maintain rapport with students with whom they have racial and cultural differences?

4. How can you use your privilege to engage in difficult conversations about race in gifted education?

5. How might you advocate for excellence in your community?

References

Coleman, A. (2019). D-STEM Equity Model: Diversifying the STEM education to career pathway. *Athens Journal of Education*. Retrieved from https://www.athensjournals.gr/education/2018-2539-AJE-STEAM.pdf

Colker, L. J. (2014). The word gap: The early years make a difference. *Teaching Young Children, 7*(3).

de Brey, C., Musu, L., McFarland, J., Wilkinson-Flicker, S., Diliberti, M., Zhang, A., Branstetter, C., & Wang, X. (2019). *Status and trends in the education of racial and ethnic groups 2018* (NCES 2019-038). Washington, DC: National Center for Education Statistics, U.S. Department of Education.

Elementary and Secondary Education Act of 1969, §142, 20 U.S.C. 863.

Every Student Succeeds Act, Pub. L. No. 114–95. (2015).

Gershenson, S., Holt, S. B., & Papageorge, N. W. (2016). Who believes in me? The effect of student-teacher demographic match on teacher expectations. *Economics of Education Review, 52*, 209–224.

Hart, B., & Risley, T. R. (2003). The early catastrophe: The 30 million word gap by age 3. *American Educator, 27*(1), 4–9.

Lakin, J. M. (2016). Universal screening and the representation of historically underrepresented minority students in gifted education: Minding the gaps in Card and Giuliano's research. *Journal of Advanced Academics, 27,* 139–149.

McFarland, J., Hussar, B., Zhang, J., Wang, X., Wang, K., Hein, S., . . . Barmer, A. (2019). *The condition of education 2019* (NCES 2019-144). Washington, DC: National Center for Education Statistics, U.S. Department of Education.

National Association for Gifted Children. (n.d.-a). *Tests & assessments.* Retrieved from https://www.nagc.org/resources-publications/ gifted-education-practices/identification/tests-assessments

National Association for Gifted Children. (n.d.-b). *What is giftedness?* Retrieved from http://www.nagc.org/resources-publications/ resources/what-giftedness

National Association for Gifted Children. (2010). *NAGC Pre-K– Grade 12 Gifted Programming Standards: A blueprint for quality gifted education programs.* Washington, DC: Author.

National Association for Gifted Children. (2018). *Key considerations in identifying and supporting gifted and talented learners: A report from the 2018 NAGC definition task force.* Washington, DC: Author.

Nicholson-Crotty, S., Grissom, J. A., Nicholson-Crotty, J., & Redding, C. (2016). Disentangling the causal mechanisms of representative bureaucracy: Evidence from assignment of students to gifted programs. *Journal of Public Administration Research and Theory, 26,* 745–757.

No Child Left Behind Act, 20 U.S.C. §6301 (2001).

Olszewski-Kubilius, P., & Clarenbach, J. (2012). *Unlocking emergent talent: Supporting high achievement of low-income, high-ability students.* Washington, DC: National Association for Gifted Children.

Olszewski-Kubilius, P., Subotnik, R. F., & Worrell, F. C. (Eds.). (2018). *Talent development as a framework for gifted education: Implications for best practices and applications in schools.* Waco, TX: Prufrock Press.

O'Neal, T. D. (2018). *The exceptional negro: Racism, white privilege and the lie of respectability politics.* Atlanta, GA: iCart Media.

Plucker, J. A., & Peters, S. J. (2016). *Excellence gaps in education: Expanding opportunities for talented students.* Cambridge, MA: Harvard Education Press.

Plucker, J. A., & Peters, S. J. (2018). Closing poverty-based excellence gaps: Conceptual, measurement, and educational issues. *Gifted Child Quarterly, 1,* 56–67.

Skelton, S. M., & Warren, C. L. (2016). *Every child, every day institute: Culturally responsive & sustaining practices in the classroom.* Retrieved from https://greatlakesequity.org/sites/default/files/20161008564_presentation.pdf

Snyder, T. D., de Brey, C., & Dillow, S. A. (2019). *Digest of education statistics 2017* (NCES 2018-070). Washington, DC: National Center for Education Statistics, Institute of Education Sciences, U.S. Department of Education.

Subotnik, R. F., Olszewski-Kubilius, P., & Worrell, F. C. (2011). Rethinking giftedness and gifted education: A proposed direction forward based on psychological science. *Psychological Science in the Public Interest, 12,* 3–54.

U.S. Department of Education. (2016). *The state of racial diversity in the educator workforce.* Washington, DC: Author.

U.S. Department of Education, Office for Civil Rights. (2014). *Civil rights data collection: 2013–14 state and national estimations.* Retrieved from https://ocrdata.ed.gov/StateNational Estimations/Estimations_2013_14

Worrell, F. C. (2010). Psychosocial stressors in the development of gifted learners with atypical profiles. In J. VanTassel-Baska (Ed.), *Patterns and profiles of low-income learners* (pp. 33–58). Waco, TX: Prufrock Press.

Yaluma, C. B., & Tyner, A. (2018). *Is there a gifted gap? Gifted education in high-poverty schools.* Washington, DC: Fordham Institute.

About the Author

April **Wells** is the gifted coordinator in Illinois School District U-46, where she facilitated the redesign of the district's gifted program in 2012–2013. April serves on the Board of Directors for the Illinois Association for Gifted Children, and she has presented at conferences, including for IAGC, the National Association for Gifted Children, the Statewide Conference for Teachers Serving Linguistically and Culturally Diverse Students, the Center for Gifted Education at William & Mary, and Vanderbilt Programs for Talented Youth. For April, gifted education is a union of personal and professional pursuits. Having grown up as a child in poverty, she recognizes the role that education plays in social mobility. Her interests focus on equity pedagogy, underrepresented learners, developing continua of gifted services, and providing instructional supports that allow students to maximize their pursuits. She received one of the 2018 Gifted Coordinator Awards from NAGC. She resides in Illinois with her husband, Charles, and their three daughters.